Olive Muriel Pink

Also by Colleen Keating and published by Ginninderra Press
A Call To Listen (Shortlisted, Society of Women Writers
NSW Book Awards 2016)
Fire on Water (Highly Commended, Society of Women Writers
NSW Book Awards 2018; Nautilus Award – Silver 2017)
Hildegard of Bingen: A poetic journey (Winner, Poetry,
and Winner, Non-fiction, Society of Women Writers NSW
Book Awards 2020; Nautilus Award, Silver, 2019)
Desert Patterns (Highly Commended, Poetry, Society of
Women Writers NSW Book Awards 2020)
Soft Gaze, with Michael Keating (Picaro Poets)
Brush of Birds (Picaro Poets)
Landscapes of the Heart, with John Egan (Picaro Poets)
Shared Footprints, with Michael Keating (Picaro Poets)
Mood Indigo, with Pip Griffin (Picaro Poets)
Mists of Time, with Decima Wraxall (Pocket Poets)

Colleen Keating

Olive Muriel Pink
Her radical and idealistic life

A poetic journey

Acknowledgements

My thanks to the members of the Women Writers Network, and Wednesday Evening Poetry group, both from Writing NSW, the Fellowship of Australian Writers Sydney city group, U3A Poetry Appreciation, and the Society of Women Writers, for their affirmation and sharing the art and friendship of poetry.

Thank you to the Varuna Residential Fellowship for space to write in the peace of the Blue Mountains.

Thanks to Ian Coleman and all who protect the Olive Pink Botanic Garden in Alice Springs where many of these poems were pondered.

Appreciation to academics Julie Marcus and Gillian Ward for their research and writings on Olive Pink.

I acknowledge the gracious access I was given to the Olive Pink archives at AIATSIS in Canberra.

Thanks to my daughter Elizabeth Keating-Jones, based in the UK, for her enthusiastic editing over the past few years and to my family for their ongoing encouragement.

Special thanks to Pip Griffin for her friendship, invaluable advice and careful edit of this work.

My loving appreciation as always to Michael for his constant presence and inspiration.

For our grandchildren and their knowledge of our country

Olive Muriel Pink: Her radical and idealistic life: A poetic journey
ISBN 978 1 76109 158 2
Copyright © text Colleen Keating 2021
Cover design: Gillian Ward (www.gmwinfodesign.com.au)

First published 2021 by
GINNINDERRA PRESS
PO Box 3461 Port Adelaide 5015
www.ginninderrapress.com.au

Contents

Foreword	13
Prologue: 1990	17
Olive the pioneer	19
1 Beginnings: 1884–1925	21
Kunanyi	23
1894	25
Growing up	27
Her father's death	29
Beyond Hobart – 1911	31
Betrothal	33
Coo-ee rings in her ear	35
A great love	38
Silence	40
A new lodestone	41
2 Through the looking glass: 1926–1928	43
First journey inland	45
Into the unknown	47
Ooldea – May 1926	48
Last day at Ooldea	51
Farewell	52
Adelaide	53
Her mother dies	54
Bohemian days	56
Marginalised by experts	57
3 Betrayal made good: 1929–1930	59
Inland Drought – 1929	61
The breaking of the drought	63
A second journey inland	65

A six-month journey inland	66
Edwards Crossing Depot	67
Sketching desert flora	69
Communication breakdown	71
Creating her own adventure	74
An awakening	75
4 The rotting frontier	**77**
Going solo	79
Alice Springs, Mparntwe	80
Journey to Darwin	81
Darwin courthouse	82
Olive on the frontier	83
A writer of letters	85
Mick Dow Dow	86
Expeditions from Alice	87
First-hand	88
Hermannsburg	89
First encounter with Albert Namatjira	91
To the star tracks	93
5 Breakthrough: 1932–1933	**95**
Back in Sydney	97
Truth – her way	99
A battle lost	101
Her vow	102
Restless	103
A breakthrough	104
Heady days	106
Final paper – seminar	108
The ANZAAS Congress 1932	110
A knitting of passions	111
Justice her sword	113

6 Research and the inland: 1933	115
Resignation	117
Third trip inland	118
High hopes	120
Tight time frame	122
A terrible mistake?	123
Ilpalentye Country	125
The corkwood tree	129
Bright star	130
Reflection	131
Whisperings from Caledon Bay	132
7 An anthropologist: 1934	135
Struggle to freedom	137
Diploma and research grant	138
A fourth journey inland	139
Research expedition	140
Yunmaji Waterhole	143
Research with the Warlpiri tribe	145
Listening	146
An opus of experience	147
Truth evades	148
8 Wings of fire: Summer 1934	151
A whispered fear	153
The rescue	154
Life-threatening journey	156
Under menacing cloud	157
Junction Waterhole	159
Wings afire	161
9 The quest: 1935–1938	165
Secular sanctuary	167
SOS Alarm	168

Melbourne Congress	169
Camouflage	171
Hobnail boots	173
Back in Alice Springs	174
Purpose with passion	175
Is it the end?	176
Back to Hobart	179
Fidelity	181
A door closes	183

10 The world in transition: 1939–1946 — 185
Return to Alice Springs	187
World War Two	191
Desert living	192
Routine at Thompson's Rockhole	194
Courage	196
Birthday	198
Hiroshima	199
Olive's world collapses	203
The escape to safety	204

11 Living in Alice Springs: 1946 — 205
A fierce campaigner	207
Home Hut	209
The courtroom	211
Justice denied	212
A fine or prison!	214

12 Friendships: 1947–1955 — 217
Generosity	219
Visitors to Home Hut	220
White Australia	222
Billy Goat Hill	224
Albert	226

Olive the Advocate	228
Bruno Dow Dow	230
Greatest honour ever	232
An uncertain future	234
Eviction	235
Inspiration	236
Thunder raining poison	238
13 Creating a garden: 1955–1973	**241**
A new fire kindles	243
A déjà vu moment	245
Creating the garden	247
My own Papinya	249
Water-wise garden	251
An acquired bath	253
Olive turns eighty	254
An enduring gardener	256
14 A first arid garden: 1974	**259**
A social justice warrior	261
Jampijinpa Yannarilyi (Johnny)	263
Being stubborn	265
The first garden party	266
15 The circle of life: 1975	**269**
The paradox of OMP	271
Joy of family	272
Dangerous Miss Pink	274
The veil	276
Autumn 1975	278
Bringing the light	280
Going home	281
Epilogue	**284**

Chronology	285
Glossary	288
Notes	299
Bibliography	318

Biography is not a finite business; it's a process, a journey. I have been researching, writing and thinking about Olive Pink for over a decade now. The discoveries that come along the way – the portraits unveiled – are very stirring.

To Indigenous communities: please be aware that some names and stories in this poetic journey are of deceased persons. For historical context, some ideas and words used reflect the period about which it is written and do not reflect modern thinking or the thoughts of the author.

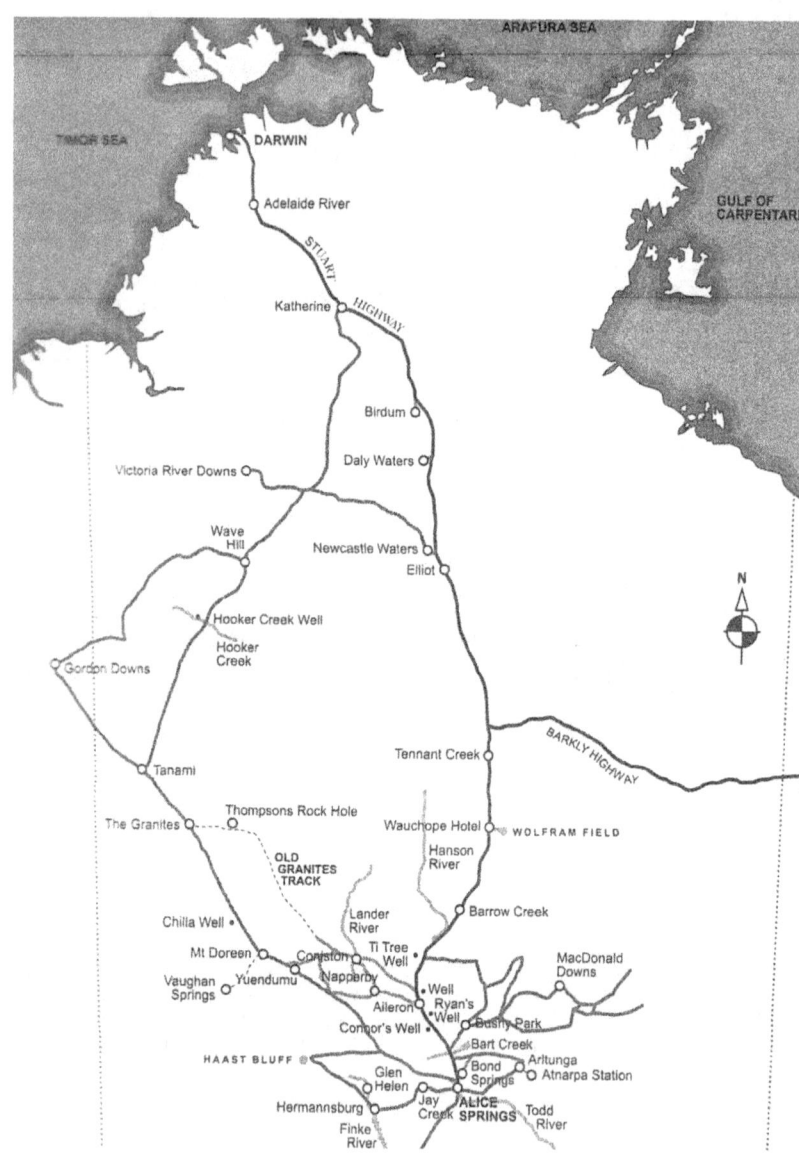

Foreword

It is only in myth that the truth about any country can be found.[1]

This poetic journey is an ode to courage, tenacity and commitment. By delving into its pages, you will be transported to a parallel realm where the gallant Olive Muriel Pink, a pioneer of our country, held a voice and vision for her time and for the future.

From the earliest memories of her Tasmanian childhood and botanical walks with her father, to the final years as curator of the drought-prone Arid Botanic Garden in Alice Springs, Olive Pink deserves to be recognised and given her place in Australian history, especially among those emerging women who confronted hardship, loss, patriarchy, rejection and invisibility.

I became curious about Olive Pink in 2009 while on a visit to Alice Springs. It intrigued me to see a woman's name enshrined on the entrance to the Botanic Garden. I asked around about Olive Pink but nobody was able to enlighten me.[2]

Back home, I became immersed in the richness of her story, a pioneer Australian woman of the first half of the twentieth century (1884–1975). Her passions and struggles unfolded before me. I found a justice warrior, an advocate for the rights of the Indigenous people, a trained anthropologist, artist, gardener, botanist and curator.

Finding research material by the anthropologist Julie Marcus and her scholarly book was invaluable. I wish to acknowledge the collections on Olive Pink in the South Australia Museum Library in Adelaide and the Northern Territory Library in Parliament House, Darwin, and especially the twenty-two labelled boxes at AIATSIS in Canberra. I realised I was not alone in my curiosity when in 2018 Gillian Ward launched her stunning literary and pictorial book on Olive's life in flowers and her garden. I like to think my poetic story complements both Julie's and Gillian's books and continues to expand our knowing of Olive and her radical and idealistic life.

Like a tiny mulga seed planted, Olive first heard about the plight of the Indigenous people from Quaker friends in Tasmania and, as a young sapling grows tall and strong with the right conditions, she looked beyond her horizon into the unknowns of study and work, following her heart into the future. Like the strong, adept mulga tree, she survived the harsh arid reality of the desert.

She lived and worked with the Warlpiri and Arrernte people and wrote her anthropological research from a position of 'inside' with empathy and imagination.[3] She became a voice for the voiceless at a time when British settlers were seeing our country through a prism of superiority. Her actions often contentious and irascible and her letters to newspapers and the government disturbed the 'Great Australian Silence'[4] that was already settling in comfortably.

Olive was strongly vocal about the 'cult of forgetfulness'[5] where what was done to the Aboriginal people was erased from memory; where the history of dispossession and destruction was being obliterated from the national narrative.

Single-minded, highly skilled, insightful and articulate, Olive Pink stuns us with her innate capacity to stand her ground.

Olive believed if the truth were known, justice would inevitably follow. She was to find her belief constantly challenged and as her pursuit of truth and justice challenged the authority of the state servants, she experienced at first hand the ways in which the voice of an unwelcome or untimely truth could be silenced.[6]

It is through this fracture that the light of Olive Pink's story shines. A woman of extraordinary sensibility and passion, not a religious woman but alive to the deeper sense of the world and its spirituality. She bore witness to the brutal injustices of her time, with her voice belittled and silenced over and over again.

In March 2020, Michael and I spent a week in Alice Springs walking in the footsteps of Olive Pink. We stayed within walking distance of the Olive Pink Botanic Garden, each morning drinking in its ambience – breakfast with the birds and wallabies in the Bean Café, walking on the set paths, marvelling at the labelled walks with their stands of arid vegetation – mulgas, hakeas, wattles, mallee and bird attracting plants, climbing to the top of Tharrarletneme (Annie Meyers Hill) with its crisp views of Mt Gillen and Caterpillar Dreaming and sitting quietly at sheltered learning nodes, reading and relaxing. Her legacy was all around us.

Today, vibrant and dedicated volunteers are integral to the life and success of the garden and are Miss Pink's concept of champions who will 'continue the protection of the garden'.

Appreciation to the Northern Territory government, who today provide a grant to employ a curator and horticulturist, and to local people who promote it to tourists as one of the most beautiful gardens for thousands of miles. All praise must go the the board of trustees, the current dynamic curator Ian Coleman and the gardeners, Bushcare groups who stay true to the mission of education, conservation, sustainability and research of Miss Pink's 'gallant ones' – the vulnerable arid flora of Central Australia.

> The past is not dead.
> It is all around us and within
> – Oodgeroo Noonuccal

The knife's between us. I turn it round
the handle to your side
the weapon made from your country's bones.
I have no right to take it.

But both of us die as our dreamtime dies
I don't know what to give you
for your gay stories, your sad eyes,
but that, and a poem, sister.

from 'Two Dreamtimes', Judith Wright, 1970

Prologue
1990

Olive the pioneer

eccentric: a person of unconventional and slightly strange views or behaviour
anthropologist: a person who studies human societies, culture and language

Olive's relatives arrive in Darwin.
They know of her heroic spirit
from family letters and stories.
In Pioneer Park they search
amongst 200 tiles
paved to honour Territorian pioneers.

They kneel by her tile, shocked –
'Olive Pink eccentric'
their ancestor the only one
described by a characteristic!

They challenge –
letters, emails, visits
representations to the highest authority.
'No' will not do for an answer.
They demand the truth.
Change the tile –
'Olive Pink anthropologist'.

Who is Olive? history asks.
She defied the silence
caused discomfort
annoyed the authorities.
Her letters shouted from the edge.
She heard budgerigar dreaming
and drummed to a different tune.

She pushed against the colonial tide.
If the answer is 'eccentric'
in her death she will be twice dismissed.

Who is Olive? history asks.
She broke the silence
her voice for the voiceless
remembered the forgetting.
She visioned justice in the courts.
Her feet knew country.
She carried red dust
under the fingernails of her heart.
She listened to elders, learnt language
wrote down stories, sketched arid plants
medicinal, nutritional, ritual.
If the answer is 'anthropologist'
in her death she will be twice honoured.

1
Beginnings
1884–1925

Kunanyi[1]

Sometimes in cloak of nature green
she stands protector
with lope and gurgle of her brooks
nurturer in the spring.

Sometimes wild and moody
she bares her teeth
stings air with icy fang
heart open, raw
whitewashed with ice and snow.

Tasmanians, in Hobart Town
live under Kunanyi's spell
a barometer
to gauge the tenor of their day.

Under her gaze, tribal groups
once walked, fished the sandy coves.
When grasses flourished
they gathered the seeds
for grinding flour
to prepare their cakes for tucker
and gathered around their fires
told stories by the stars.

Under Kunanyi's gaze white sails
brought convicts, chain-ganged
for barracks at Port Arthur.
Their cries still pierce the dark
beyond screech of crow, howl of wind.

And under her gaze thin, bedraggled women
were hassled at rifle point
to a cold-cell gaol, a female factory,
where their moans deadened the bark of dogs.

Under her gaze blood flowed
at Risdon Cove.
Kunanyi, whispered to silence.

And eighty years on –
in a modest house midst autumnal chill
and sway of gold-leafed trees
under her gaze
with her grandmother as midwife
Olive Muriel Pink is born.

1894

In the foothills of Kunanyi
Olive, a lithe and curious ten-year-old
holds her father's hand –
watches an echidna cross their path.

She skips ahead
weaves in and out of spindly, twisted roots
stunted scrub, boulders of schist and basalt.

She calls out to her father and his friend,
'A new wildflower!'
The three of them crouch
before purple spread of pea-like petals.
Olive traces her finger
along the narrow leaves
points at the stem's alternate nodes,
'They are tough like leather.'
'Yes,' her father says,
'this helps to conserve their water.'

He passes her a well-worn plant book.[2]
She thumbs pages, identifies the sketch
sounds the words out loud, 'Hovea montana.'
He proudly pats her plaited hair.

Tree ferns canopy the mountain path.
They ramble beside the Derwent River
a wildflower haven.

Olive doesn't mind which way they go
as long as her father is with her
exploring and investigating.
'My little Alice,'
he teases,
'curiouser and curiouser.'³

Growing up

Olive has her father's keen eyes
her mother's shy, artistic ways.
As a pebble dropped in a pond
nature and art ripple out around her –
books and learning, her touchstone.

Teachers, schooled in English ways
inspire her learning with drawing, etiquette
scarf dancing, speech and deportment.

She absorbs a Quaker slant
with its pillar of social justice
and whispered stories of Aborigines –
their persecution in defence of country.[4]

At college, the Art Department buzzes.
Olive arrives early, ties her pinafore over
her white Edwardian dress, prepares
the ink wells, easels, paints
sets out drawing paper, makes the pot of tea.
Lucien Dechineux, her lecturer,[5]
enthuses her. With each pencil stroke
Olive's drawings come alive.

A family friend, Mary Walker
returns from art studies in London.
She brings a collection of European art.[6]
Olive's face glows
over paintings and sculptures
she could never imagine.

Her vision widens to sculpture class
and teaching art.

She sits across the room
from another student, Harold Southern.
His artistic skill and smile catch her eye.
Harold, his sister Muriel and Olive
form a threesome at weekends
searching out wildflowers and sketching
for hours. They submit paintings
for the annual exhibition.
Olive wins!
The thrill of her first success in art
whets her quest for more.

Her father's death

The blow of death strikes at Olive's very being.
Without her father she is pale, bereft,
a bird deprived of its song.
Her love of drawing and new career of teaching art
are meaningless. Little consolation
when her sketch *Sunflowers*
is acclaimed by the Tasmanian Art Society.
Now it means nothing.

Where is his strong hand
leading her on to new adventures?
She can still hear his deep melodious voice
singing around the piano.
She recalls with a shiver
the sleek smell of his black hair.

Frozen like her mountain
as Antarctic air whips sharply
a wipeout of emotion
a wipeout of energy and ambition.
Windblown like Hobart town
on the edge of the world
lashed by regret
her centre cannot hold.
Grief wrenches at her. She wilts.
A wild flower plucked from its source.

Leaves on the maple curl, weep.
Even the minnow in the nearby creek
dive deep. Her dreams have turned to stone.

Sometimes when the shadow
of the mountain deepens
she ponders,
'Maybe it is not the mountain
that saddens me,
perhaps I sadden the mountain.'

Beyond Hobart – 1911

Her brother Eldon is left to support
the family. With only modest funds
and jobs scarce
he is lured by farming opportunities
and urges his mother and Olive
to sail with him to the growing city of Perth.[7]

Olive knows the danger
of losing what she has[8]
yet she is enlivened
by sailing on the high seas.

She stands on the top deck.[9]
As horizons fall she marvels
at a bigger world.
The sky stretches forever
over the southern ocean.

Her smile returns with the bubble
and chatter of new friends.
At night dripping stars encircle the ship
and the south winds clear
every dark corner of her mind.

Olive writes, many years later,
'It was all such fun.
I bowled the Captain (for a duck)
helped by the roll of the ship
in the Bight – when playing deck cricket.'[10]

In Perth the family settle on the land.
Eldon struggles to farm –
drought, workers lost to the gold rush
failing crops, money scarce.

Olive bursts with new energy,
'I'll start teaching,
rent a studio in St Georges Terrace.
It's what I prefer anyway!'
Her mother hesitates
but hears her determination.

Olive walks tall. Her steps confirm
a new sense of purpose.
She sees possibilities.
Her hands with wings of hope
design her first plaque.
She proudly affixes it to the studio door
traces the gold lettered words
stands back and whispers
'Miss Olive Pink, Artist.'
Her spirit spirals into the wind
and echos around the town.[11]

Betrothal

Wildflowers quicken
Olive's curiosity –
colours, sounds, smells
garish bright light
crisp, ocean-sharp air.
'Western Australia is a happy hunting ground
for the wild-flower lover,'
she writes in a Sydney journal.[12]

Walking on the banks of the Swan River
satchel loaded with paper, pencils, paint
Olive captures the trees and birds
commits to paper, nature around her.

Each weekend she walks in the park
sketches and writes.
Her articles, published in the East
enrich and affirm.

Then a chance meeting with an old friend –
Harold Southern, now an analytical chemist.
He suggests they picnic and paint.
'Just like old times,' he adds.
A blush rises, flames her face.
Her eyes light up.

Just out of town,
the dry land bursts into a blaze
of wildflowers,
inspiring their palettes.

One Sunday afternoon
their world bursts into richer colour.
Leaning in to mix the water paint
they brush arms.
Olive feels a tingle. Goosebumps prickle.
Her face flushes scarlet
brighter than the Kangaroo Paw
that abounds on the red earth.

In shock, they move apart.
They share a long gaze
embrace and know
what they have always known
since Hobart days.

In the shade of the river paperbarks –
a shy kiss. A oneness is theirs.
She loves his laughter.
Now it is part of her.

Coo-ee rings in her ear

Olive's steps are light
her world is light.
Yet beyond the edge
the very distant edge of her world
1914 rumbles in the darkness.

'England is at war, hence the Empire is at war.'

Overnight, posters appear –
'We fight for King and country.
Boys, come over here, you are wanted.
Every young man is called forward.
Australians arise, Save us from shame.
Coo-ee, won't you come.'[13]

Olive stares at the signs. Seethes.
Coo-ee rings like tinnitus.
The slogans tattoo her mind.
'This is propaganda,' she tells her mother.
'The posters are everywhere.
Look, even this magazine
in colour glorifying war.'

Olive wants to tear down every poster.
Others do. More go up.

Harold joins a long enlistment queue
at Swan Barracks, arrives
at her studio in uniform
expecting pride to flush her face.

Shock in her eyes
she steps back,
shakes her head,
'No, no. Never, not you.' She covers her face
her hands muffle a distraught cry.
Anger rises.
'You can't leave your job.'

He makes to put his arms around her.
She pushes him away, shouts,
'This is not our war. It is over there.
We are pacifists!'
Her hand shakes. Her voice slows, deepens,
'It is a far away war. Over there!
We don't even know what they are fighting for!'
Olive pulls her jacket closer.
'I can't believe we see this so differently.'

She turns away.
Her shoulders slump, she stumbles
along a path that yesterday was smooth.

Choking back her sobs she rushes
to her mother,
'How can I stop this? Turn time back!
It is all out of control.'
She falls into the armchair
holds her throbbing head.

In the streets
anticipation stirs, flags
chatter… 'Our boys sailing.'
Olive is numb,
this euphoria is anathema to her.

Harold waits for her return from work.
His last visit!
Olive makes the tea, sits down.
He gives her two of his paintings,[14]
'This is my best for you to remember me.'
Her eyes mist with memories of their days
by the Swan River
painting, laughing, planning.

Her broken voice finds its timbre,
'I can never agree with war.
Yet we are in love,' she whispers.
Despite herself she almost smiles.
'And I must say you look mighty handsome
in uniform. I need a photo of you in this light.
Now I must wait for your return.
Then we will be together.'

Hundreds of handsome young men
bid farewell, impatient to sail
for the adventure of their lives
on the *Ascanius,* bound for the Middle East.[15]
Their mascot a hidden joey!

A great love

Olive and her mother sail for Sydney
for a house and garden in Greenwich.
Olive begins study –
Town Planning at Sydney University.[16]
Postcards from Egypt generate laughter
as they read of Harold's sore rear
from the fun of camel riding.

Then silence.

Rekindled friendship
with Harold's sister Muriel
brings solace.
They talk of Tassie days
of Harold and growing up.
They sketch and paint
sell greeting cards and calendars.

In May worrying news seeps in –
the word 'Gallipoli' murmured.
Telegrams begin to arrive
and when received
doors close with grief.

One mournful autumn day
when leaves fall down like tears
Muriel moans the worst news…
…killed
early…one of the first mornings
…on the shore of Gallipoli.[17]
Silence its own lament.

Harold's absence questions life.
The only answer, the rustle
and crackle of brown leaves.

Back with her mother
Olive lives deep, numbing days.
She holds her only photo close
hoping for a telegram
to say it was all a mistake.

Giddy, light-headed
she collapses, clutching her chest.
Her doctor diagnoses a strained heart valve
from severe shock.[18]

Silence

Silence of friends lost in their own grief.
Silence of her cries swallowed
in a deep ocean of sadness.

The injured are being brought home.
Olive joins the Red Cross
is on the wharf
to meet the first hospital ship
to berth in Sydney.
Maybe…just maybe…

Carriers take stretchers from the ship.
She sees white faces and eyes gripped
in fear and pain.
Olive recalls his eyes searching hers
the brush of his hand giving her his paintings[19]
his warm breath on her skin as he whispered,
'A gift for you to remember me till I return.'
and how her heart beat fast.

A new lodestone

The grim spectre of injustice
towards Aboriginal tribes
taunts Olive out of her grief
jolts her from self pity.
Like a silk petticoat pulled over her hair
the air is static in its darkness.
It bleeds through a colander of whitewash words
– progress, jobs, growth.
Its handprint blood-red.

The newly established League of Nations[20]
speaks of cruelty, slavery, shootings inland.
Olive, seeded by her Quaker influence
joins the Association for the Protection
of Native Races. She is compelled
to see for herself. 'Curiouser and curiouser'
she hears her father's voice of encouragement.

She writes to Daisy Bates[21]
and is invited to visit –
'Take a train to Ooldea.[22]
You will be collected.'

The newest atlas at the city library reveals
a map of vast empty spaces
patterned with unfamiliar markings.

Her finger snakes along
the new train track
seeking the strange name Ooldea.
She catches her breath in delight.

The risks of a journey into the unknown –
a woman travelling alone
taking time off from her job
leaving her mother.

The lodestone of justice spurs her on.
Nothing will stop her.

2
Through the looking glass
1926–1928

First journey inland

Olive steams out of Adelaide.
The rail cuts a parallel
into the skin of the country
on the Tea and Sugar rattler[1]
ploughs a straight line west
to the edge of the Nullarbor.

Sweat trickles down the nape of her neck.
Hot, sticky air hazes the clanking beat
of metal on metal.

Her quarter-open window crawls with flies.
She peers out through the dust
squints at the country –
tangerine and ochre earth
scatter of grey stunted vegetation
splurge of endless sky.

Olive thrills at the landscape
and its unfamiliar flora
in this harsh wild land.

She reaches for her sketch pad.
Her hand moves excitedly.
She notes,
'The fleshy leaves of mallee glinted in sunlight
…red soil covered in quaint grass tufts
like pincushions.'[2]

At rail sidings
they refill water
unload mail and supplies.

A huddle of Aborigines
silent and subdued
watch with inquisitive eyes.
Some purchase supplies
from the store carriage.
Children wave to her train
as it slinks on its way.

Into the unknown

A bellow of brakes.
The guard pulls the door open
and sets the steps.
A crowd of flies and smell of ash
her Ooldea welcome.[3]

Olive climbs down
amid excited chatter of Aborigines.
Some jostle to fetch her luggage.

A tall, erect figure steps forward.
Daisy Bates – Kabbarli[4]
in high-collared white shirt
black coat, long black skirt and black boots.
Olive is captivated.
She takes the white-gloved hand
extended in greeting.

Olive stands among Aborigines
listens to the strangeness of their speech.
They reach out to touch her.
She can't understand their tongue
but feels as one with their smiles.
A little girl hands her a note of welcome
and a large jug of water.
Olive drinks. Water trickles down her face.

At forty-two years old
Olive's eyes gleam as she looks out
on her new world.

Ooldea – May 1926

They follow a red sandy track
peppered with blue-grey saltbush
amidst chatter and laughter
to their camp of brushwood boughs
and store tents braced in the mallee scrub
– blue-leaved and greyish green
against a rocky outcrop.

At Daisy's behest
Olive opens a store-tent fold.
A glimmer of softness crosses her face.
She wrote later
'A guest room here in this far away place,
already I feel at home.'[5]
She runs her hand over the English linen
made up on the stretcher
smells freshness of towels
and sprigs of quandong flowers
inhales aroma of a lavender pincushion
and admires Daisy's touch of luxury –
a bar of violet soap.
'Everything had been done so charmingly
to welcome me – even a comfy chair
in my tent – with arms to it.'[6]

After billy tea with lemon
and real camp oven raisin cake
Daisy prepares Olive for the desert
with white gloves
and her first fly-netted hat.

They cook each evening at dusk.
By fire's warmth and dance of light
they share – tête-à-tête.
Laughter rings on the night air.
Daisy's community, sitting
beyond the ring of light
listen and watch.

Before dawn they are out walking.
They sit on a low rise with notebooks
sketching pad and pencils
capture the brooding colours of the sky
in the glow of morning.
'When I stepped out of my tent
everything would be bejewelled
with glistening dewdrops
– even the spider webs –
the sky a translucent blue
and silhouetted against it like a frieze
in green, blue, red, and yellow,
great numbers of parrots
of three different kinds…'[7]

Olive looks around amazed
at the vibrancy.
She sketches the landscape, flora, birds
the faces of children
who watch and giggle close by.
She wants to capture every tiny piece
of this living world.

Daisy walks Olive around her garden –
green beans, tomatoes, smell of herbs
desert flowers. Olive crushes a leaf
inhales sharply
marvels at this garden in the arid earth.

Olive is intrigued by the patter
of Aboriginal talk
and watches Daisy communicate
in many dialects.[8]
Fascinated, Olive longs
to emulate such skills.

Searching out words and their meaning
becomes a joyous part of her day.
She wrote later
'I listen to their language
but my attempts
make the children laugh more and more.'[9]

Her old world drifts away.
Her new world is all that matters –
these people
this country.

Last day at Ooldea

Olive wakes early, steps out, ventures
further than before. The arc of dawn flexes
an awakening blush.
Some of the children follow
at a discreet distance.

An outcrop of rock beckons.
She sits with her sketchpad in hand
gazes out over the edge of the Nullarbor
sighs with content.
The land sprawls in its gown
of deep mauve
a sleeping beauty surrendering
to wakefulness.
The kiss of first sun
sears into her memory.

Out of silence
budgerigars swing overhead.
Dawn will bring their chatter.
For now they circle –
their salute
fading into the distance.

'This desert is alive'
she tells Daisy later
'yet the emptiness astounds me.
The earth has a voice.
It whispers in my heart,
feels like my home.'[10]

Farewell

Adults gift carved wooden artefacts.
The children offer bunches of wild flowers
with the sprinkle of tiny yellow daisies.
'They clap, sing their chants,
with string dances rippling to their toes
a poetry of motion on the red earth.'[11]
Dust is whipped up by the arriving steam train.
She assures the children 'I'll be back' –
and treasures the shine of their smiles.

Olive climbs the train's steep steps
amidst smoke, ash and heat
pauses on the upper step
waves her white-gloved hand.

The Ooldea Range stretches away
pale indigo against the skyline.
She takes a long glance at the community
of full-blood Aborigines – innocent
even as they are shadowed
by the threats of colonialism.

As the train steams off
Olive realises that in six weeks
this country has scuff-marked a track
into her heart.

Flocks of galahs and Mitchell cockatoos
feeding in flowering mallee
create a flotilla of flying colours.
Her eyes mist to their farewell flashes
of mauve and green.

Adelaide

In Adelaide, Olive strides
with new-found confidence
sees her future with fresh eyes.
Her face brown and sun-dried
her hands now adept
in outback needs and challenges
she is a new version of herself.
She has savoured the taste of red earth.

Before her return train to Sydney
she visits the Adelaide Museum
making friends and new contacts.
She donates artefacts and plant specimens
and desert flora sketches.
The Anthropological Society of South Australia
inspires her to set up a group in New South Wales.

Olive writes of the startling landscape
its spread and textures of life.
She speaks of the Aborigines caught
in the grab for their land.

The experience and new knowledge
sharpens her words
launches her voice –
and for the rest of her life
she will not be silenced.

Her mother dies

Olive returns to work
as draughtsman for the railways.[12]
Memories of her desert holiday
crowd in
overshadow her routine.
She remembers the people
eyes dulled with loss of land
yet bubbly with laughter
when she attempted words
in their language.

A sea fret of illness
engulfs her mother.
Olive takes six months leave
to care for her.
One night she wakes in panic
gulps for air, heavy with fear.
Olive would give up all her dreams
to avoid the inevitable.

Fourteen happy years
with her mother in Sydney
falter
beyond what she can bear.

The wait between breaths.
Long aching silences
creeping in through every gasp
to emptiness, desolation, loss.[13]
Olive writhes against reality.

All seems meaningless.
House, garden, family, furniture.
Her only solace, desert memories
and her vow one day to return.

Bohemian days

Loss leaves a hole in a person
and holes like to be filled
even as gentle drops of rain
fill an empty pond.[14]

Her interests in anthropology
her love of art and sketching
and flamboyant personality
flourish in Sydney's Bohemian circle.
Weekends see her bushwalking
sketching, painting wildflowers –
her gentle drops of rain.

Olive's artist friend Adrien Feint
creates a bookplate for her –
a lithe woman, naked
intent on her journey up a dark
mountain, her fired torch
carried high she stands on her truth
striding distant mountains to beauty.[15]

Olive glues her bookplate
into her books
proud of its brazen show.
She suggests to one friend
'Enjoy the book
stick the bookplate page together
if it bothers you.'[16]

Marginalised by experts

When a group of academics
from the museum and university meet[17]
Olive lobbies for an Anthropological Society.
'I've seen its value in Adelaide.'
She says in a passionate voice,
'We need a voice to represent
the interests of Aborigines to the government.'

It is 1928 with whispers of sanctioned massacres.
Olive co-opts her friend Radcliffe-Brown
to lead their group as a founding member.
Olive believes he will be uncompromising.

Proud of her first-hand knowledge
her confidence flourishes.
She writes of her recent experiences.
Eager to impress, she contributes to debate
listens intently to other radical thinkers.[18]

The first volume of their new journal
Mankind arrives.
It records their beginnings
meetings, shared ideas.
Olive feels a buzz of anticipation.

Her hand trembles as she opens it.
Her eyes run down the list of contents.
Her pride becomes indignation.
She lets the journal slither to the ground.
Her article is not included.
No mention of her name.

Olive paces up and down.
Her heart aches.
She has been ignored.

One essay suggests
full-blooded Aborigines from the interior
be exhibits to celebrate
the opening of the Harbour Bridge.[19]
There is no mention
of her vehement opposition.

At the next meeting, her voice indignant
she rages against ignorance and inhumanity.

They accuse her of emotionalism
and sentimentality. She realises
they seek to silence her.

Rage becomes resolution.
Defiance her answer.
She will be heard!

3
Betrayal made good
1929–1930

Inland Drought – 1929

Cattle drives – money driven.
Season in, season out
red dust creeps into every crevice.
The country is in drought.

Crank and dusty tramp
of four hundred bullocks
pounds the land hard.
Cattle have no respect for sacred sites
no respect for waterholes, grass plantings
nor sixty-thousand-year history.

Settlers demand from the land
more than it can give –
whip and lash it into submission.
The pick and shovel world
of cameleer and gold prospector
gives way to dynamite.
Claypan squatters
race to take up second-choice country.

Enter the fray – Randal Stafford
distinguished British stockman
and his mates Brooks and Morton.[1]
Stafford names his station Coniston
disdains the local tribes of Aborigines
living on the outskirts of his land –
'Labour their only value,' he states
and issues daily rations
well aware of the crucial results.[2]

The land collapses.
The Yurrkuru Soak dries.
Starvation wails.
A land parched, a people crippled.[3]

The breaking of the drought

1930 rings in a new decade.
Sydney newspapers report
'Parched lands soaked with rain,
coming alive. Acres of wildflowers!'
Olive's imagination is fired.
The inland beckons.

Shadows of the
Coniston Massacre[4]
seep into substrata of city consciousness.
Darkness of its message
crowds Olive's mind. She searches
for facts, confronts a pall of silence.[5]

Distracted at her draughting job
a shiver of fear chills her.
Whispers of shootings inland.
She is haunted by the eyes
of the children in Ooldea.

At home she wakes
in the foetal position
breathing rapidly, troubled
by dehumanising stories.
She is drowning
in the rip of a disturbing world.

A raft to the rescue
in the person of A.P. Elkin.[6]
His writings evoke
a concern for the plight
of the inland Aborigines!

In their correspondence Olive finds
a kindred spirit. Her spirits are buoyed.

She learns he is going inland
resolves to meet and travel with him.

A second journey inland

Her second trip inland is birthed.
Olive plans to meet Pastor Elkin
in the busy town of Oodnadatta
busy, as it is the end of the rail line.
She will observe how he hires camels and guides
and travel with him into the country.

A single woman
she seizes the opportunity –
Elkin's experience
a safety net for her dreams.

Six months leave with free rail pass[7]
and her small inheritance
she boards the steam train
to Melbourne then Adelaide
the gateway to her inland world.
Olive pinches herself.
This is real!

A six-month journey inland

In Adelaide no message awaits her!
Letters to Elkin unanswered.
'I am not worried,' she tells friends.
'There is no hurry.
We plan to meet in Oodnadatta.[8]
I have several stops planned along the way.'
Her plan – to travel slowly
camp in places, meet Aborigines,
study and sketch the local flora.

Her Museum friends
equip her for the journey[9]
camping gear, supplies
and specimen pouches, urging her
to bring back plants for the Museum.

Joie de vivre tingles down her spine.
Her step is light and determined.
She would sever day from night
rather than turn back now.

Edwards Crossing Depot

Olive revels in the rickety ride
of the old train.[10]
She smiles, hums to herself
taps the dust-fogged window to its beat.

A burnished arid land opens up.
She breathes deeply.
As the train passes, pink and grey galahs
catch the rush of air then tilt
and wheel away filling the sky.

In a spume of steam and ash
brakes screech a metallic halt
at the Edwards Crossing Depot —[11]
her first planned stay.
Olive sees a few stone buildings
a dozen huts, some tin sheds
a gang of fettlers, station hands and wives
an outer circle of Aborigines –
workers, beggars, fringe dwellers
all curious to meet
this visiting white woman.

Heat, ash and flies greet her
along with Horrie Simpson, a fettler.
Tall, broad-shouldered with delicate
though calloused hands.
He throws his head back freely
laughs at the smallest joke.

Curious about plants and drawing
(once caught by his boss sketching a flower)
he is put in charge
of the visiting lady
who wants to sketch the plants.
Horrie later wrote,
'A lady artist by the name of Miss Pink was coming.
We men had bets on her looks, what colour hair…
Then this day I saw a small, sedately dressed woman
step off the carriage. Streaks of grey
were already showing in her dark hair.
She put out her gloved hand and said in a cultured voice,
"I'm very happy to meet you."
I knew I had a new friend and it proved so
during the long years ahead.'[12]

Sketching desert flora

The week folds into itself.
Meals with the group in the mess
then Horrie and Olive set out
with sketchpads, pens, specimen pouches
her long skirt shushing the red earth.
Wonderful spreads of wildflowers
bring them close.
She savours the way
he points out lizard tracks –
his awareness of the land
complementing her artistry.

At close of day, alone next to her tent
– set behind a shed for privacy –
Olive marvels at the big sky
its clouds like white streaks
trailing to the edge
a hazy mirage.
She takes in the brash spills of light.
Her eyes come alive to the land.
She listens to its deep silence
behind the bird chatter
by the railway water tanks.

Calm seeps into her very being.
Within this land she draws
walks on, sits on
beats a fragile heart.

She says later,
'I have met in Horrie
a courtly bush gentleman
and I can tell you
it is hard not to fall in love
with this place.'[13]

Communication breakdown

Olive chugs along, her slow train
blows smoke, rattles with anticipation
Oodnadatta its destination.
Pastor Elkin will meet her
ready for their adventure.

For now the journey is enough.
She marvels at the vastness.
Grassy plains undulate in emerald folds
like the swell of an ocean.

A squeal of brakes heralds arrival.
She checks her reflection in the dusty window
dons her netted hat
checks her high-necked blouse and brooch
climbs down the ladder
and searches the crowd
for the bird-like figure of Pastor Elkin.

In the deafening hiss of steam
Olive is shocked by the bustle
shouting of orders and the swarm of flies.
Afghans and Aborigines unload
and load supplies and mail.

She gags at the smell of dried sweat
fermenting horse and camel dung
around tethered animals.

Aborigines huddle in scant shade
tall, dark-skinned, thin so thin!
Some swagger in work gangs.
Some sit with begging hands.

Not one familiar face.

The sun blazes.
Olive's agitation swells.
Her breathing shallows.
'Nothing to do
but to wait in hope of a message'
she tells herself.

Then the news filters in –
the expedition left days ago.

'What? Gone? With guides?'

The expedition has left without her.[14]
The knot in her gut spurs
her into action.
She stores her luggage, hires a bed
for the night. At the guest house
she writes her rage, her hurt, her betrayal
and has it sent to Elkin.

Her head thumps from the intense heat.
At twilight she walks outside.
The Musgrave Ranges are aglow
in wonderful tones of blue and indigo.

She breathes a long slow sigh
hears her father's murmur, repeats it aloud,
'Well, tomorrow is another day.'

Creating her own adventure

Alone. The cold sting
of a strange place
the smell of Oodnadatta clothes her.
A young Pitjantjatjara man
princely, tall, slender
his scarified skin shining
in the brash light
stands solitary
shaded by a bright red bean tree.
Their eyes meet.

He approaches, bows,
taps his chest
'Nunguri.'

He holds out a stone in the palm of his hand
for her to buy.
'*Tjurunga*,' he mumbles proudly.

Olive intuits its sacredness
smiles and quickly replies,
'If you take me to see your country
from where it comes, I will buy it.'

An awakening

Before dawn the next day they set out.
Her new friend Nunguri leads her
onto his country.
Olive has her sketchbook in hand
and a new lightness in her step
immersed in a Pitjantjatjara world
still untouched by Europeans.
She takes in the rocky hills
red flinty earth, arid plants
and harsh ochre country.

Nunguri sells her the *tjurunga,*
a woman's *tjurunga*
connected to the hakea flower
an ancestor of this place.[15]
He tells her about the plants.
She scribbles in her notebook
sketches the mulga in full blossom
collects specimens for the museum.
Deep in country Nunguri gathers
some of the men. In the shade of a *wiltjas*
Olive watches them dance and chant
to the rhythm of their breathing
and heartbeat of the earth.
'Quivering leg muscles attest
to their deep fervour,' she later writes.
Olive is awed, sparked by a mystery
into something unknown, unknowing.

Their dark eyes gleam.
Their story and language
reveal the core of who they are.
Olive senses their union
and relation with the earth.

The final day in Oodnadatta dips
into the shadow of the Musgrave Range.
Quiet whispers buoy her.
She writes later,
'The people are aware of oneness –
their wellbeing interconnected with the earth.
How this desert country is alive
this tribal world is alive.'[16]

4

The rotting frontier[1]

The wind is blowing and our old song is broken
– Barry Hill

Going solo

Olive takes two weeks
in Pitjantjatjara country sketching
and sitting with people.

While the pain of betrayal remains raw
she makes the decision to join
the new train for the journey north
to the Finke Siding camp
by the Lilla Creek.
Her sketchpad empowers her to make
friendly contact with the local people.
She sits in the sparse shade
of spindly mulga sketching plants.

Her thoughts come alive.
'I have new confidence from this trip
my vision is expanded
I have been let down by Pastor Elkin
but I am here.
It is my dream come true:
hardly possible for a lone woman.
I am here.
Rather than return I will go on.'[2]

She travels to the end of the train line –
the fledgling town of Alice Springs.[3]

Alice Springs, Mparntwe

Two streets stand parallel
cosy with small dwellings
beside the Todd River.
Grey gums snake their way
along the dry river bed.
Corellas wing their way above.

She notes, 'All the whites in town,
all the blacks outside on reserves
beyond the Telegraph Station
near a permanent waterhole.'[4]

Aborigines around town
are dull-eyed and lethargic.
Her flashes of anger
even a sting of tears are her reaction.
She finds the town gaol is packed with blacks
who are used to collect night soil and rubbish
with enslaved pay.
She is disgusted to realise
some are paid in alcohol!

Olive's questions bring no answers.

In her mind a life formulates –
a journey with Aboriginal people
a journey for Aboriginal justice
a lifetime struggle to change attitudes.

Journey to Darwin

Olive hears of an imminent court case
involving two Aboriginal men in Darwin
She resolves to see things first hand.

She walks to the Telegraph Station
studies the territory map
traces the journey with her finger.
The clerk shakes his head, presses his lips
with a not-possible look.
'I must go.
I can do this.
The mail truck to Birdum,
then pick up the freight train into Darwin.[5]
It is possible!'
Olive readies to place herself in the firing line.
Nothing will thwart her determination.

Three days in the mail truck.
She chokes on dust. Heat exhausts her.
A journey needled with spinifex tracks
an unknown desert of massive termite mounds
and boulders that seem dropped from the heavens.
'This world never ceases to amaze me.
Oh, I wish I could stop to sketch.'

Every stop crawls with heat and flies
then two more days by freight train.
Aboriginal people watch along the way
children wave the train onwards.
Olive peers at lush vegetation, cascading water
into a wet, humid, tropical world.

Darwin courthouse

Outside the courthouse
her steps falter.
She feels exposed.
Her long dress clings and sticks.

Aborigines huddle in scant shade.
At the entrance she gasps
holds a hanky to her nose.
The heavy air could be rung out
like a wet mop.
Rusting ceiling fans creak.

Olive on the frontier[6]

Guards drag in two young Aborigines
chained wrists and legs.
There is the sweaty smell of fear.
Olive braces against the clank
of metal on metal.

'How do you plead?' the magistrate asks.

The young boys, heads hung on dark shoulders
are pushed to their feet.
The interpreter (policeman-accuser)
cocky in blue shirt
and khaki shorts
stands, coughs, pulls up long socks.
The boys mumble in language.
The policeman calls out, 'Guilty.'
Each query the policeman
answers for them
in white-man-pidgin talk.

Each day Olive sits in a wooden pew
close to an open window
every sense soaked in shock.
She feels pressure around her chest.
Her frustrated fist drums the windowsill.
Often her anger is too much to bear.
She calls out in a loud voice,
'Shame, shame, shameful…not British justice!'
She takes the warning
waits
then shouts again.

Finally the sweating magistrate
shrugs his shoulders. 'Take them down –
guilty of murder.' He bangs the hammer.
Smacks the book closed.

Olive stands, mouth open, heart racing.
A month of court cases,
a month of Darwin's humid weather.

Is fighting injustice a battle lost?
She packs her rage
journeys back to Alice
vows to seek retribution and justice.

A writer of letters

At her lodgings
Olive sits at a rickety wooden table
her hair wound into a loose knot
her burden heavy and urgent
lips set in defiance.

Paper meant for sketching
becomes writing paper.
She dips her pen in black ink
angrily writes letters
to politicians, newspapers
people at every level of power.[7]

Passionate words in varied size
sprawl across the page
embellished in coloured inks.
Deafness about this 'rotting frontier'
will not be condoned!

Mick Dow Dow

In Alice the milder days revive her.
Annie Meyers, her landlady tells her
some guides are in town.
Under a shady gum by the dry Todd
two Aboriginal guides, Mick and Bruno[8]
rest their camels after an expedition
with a camera crew.

Olive watches from a distance
then with hesitant steps walks towards them.
They stand, take off their hats.
Shirtless, their dark skin glistens
in the afternoon light
with scarification and cicatrix.
She looks up into their smiling faces
puts out a strong hand.
A surge of warmth rushes up her arm.
'Miss Pink is my name.
I was wondering if I could hire
you and the camels.'

Expeditions from Alice

Mick Dow Dow and his brother Bruno
agree to be her guides
hire camels, help her buy supplies.

She is amazed at their knowledge
and command of English.

A late spring dawn.
Mick helps her up onto a camel
packed with supplies.
Her long skirt ruffles out
as she adjusts her black fly net.

'What if Pastor Elkin could see me now!
I am doing what I came to do.
A woman alone.
This is a dream come true,'
she tells Mick.
'It is like I am an anthropologist – my dream.'

Slowly their expedition heads
into the MacDonald Ranges
west of Alice Springs.

High on a camel swaying to and fro
with a straight back and broad smile
Olive rides into her future.

First-hand

Mick admires Olive's curiosity.
Her readiness to listen encourages him.
She records everything she hears and sees
learns of his clan affiliations
his totemic identity and rituals.

She records Aranda language
lists names of plants with Arrerente words
their nutrition and healing powers.
For nearly a month they travel and camp
through Glen Helen and Stanley Chasm
their next camp –
the Hermannsburg Mission Station.

Hermannsburg[9]

Olive is suspicious of mission stations.
In her recent readings she dubbed
all mission stations imperial and intrusive.

Pastor Albrecht greets her
while Mick Dow Dow sets up camp.

Olive and the pastor share human concerns
for the local people. Both nod seriously
on the sanctity of waterholes
and the essential connect with their land.
Olive welcomes their warm exchange.
She feels his support
promises on her return to Sydney
to lobby against further threats
to land and water
by miners and pastoralists.[10]

The next day at the station
she sees stolen sacred stones
on display and for sale – as curios.

Horrified, face flushed
she confronts the pastor.
'Only an owner can sell a *tjurunga*.[11]
This is theft.
It means spiritual devastation
for the future of their culture.'

He shrugs his shoulders.
'They are of no more importance than idols
no significance. Like the "golden calf",'[12]
he flicks his fingers,
'they will be destroyed –
our Christian message is key to survival.'

Olive is stunned, shakes her head
walks away.

First encounter with Albert Namatjira

Just on the edge of the Mission Station
Olive encounters an Arrernte man
sitting alone in the sparse shade
of a white bark ghost gum.
Closer, she sees he is painting.
His old army coat and slouch hat
make him look older than his early thirties.

He smiles up at her, a proud glint in his eye
as she looks down at his painting of country.
'Albert, Albert Namatjira.'[13]
He reaches up to shake her hand.
Olive looks at his canvas
gazes, her mouth open in awe
like one seeing into the colours
of a monarch butterfly for the first time.

She peers out at the country, the red earth
the white trunks of gnarled eucalypts
the hills lying like a goddess
in a blue and purple gown
and looks back at his canvass.
His joyful brushstokes speak to her.

Later she says she 'recognised his talent as
she recognises the aroma of crushed sage'.

Over the next days she walks with him
sketch pad and pens in hand.
The Victorian-dressed Miss Pink
and a softly spoken Albert
sit scanning his Arrernte country.

They find common ground conversing
on hills, valleys, rocks and trees
her intuitive skills enhanced in his presence.

Fearful his work will flit away
Olive buys two of his paintings.
'Good value for money, you get four
for the price of two.' He turns them over
'Look, painting on the back.'
Olive smiles as she packs the paintings away.
Albert Namatjira promises to visit her
when he comes to Alice.

To the star tracks

An odd group gather around their camp.
Olive, Bruno, Mick, their wives and families.
Evening coolness seeps along the creek bed.
Olive hears the sound of night being called in
camels and hiss of kettle as the fire comes to life.

A moonless night, stars at their brightest
they sit in stillness by the slow warm embers
gazing at infinity.

Mick points at dark spaces
outlined in stars
draws his finger in shapes
– an empty curve that is the coolamon
from where a baby star fell – the crater is yonder.
He points to the emu, the dark space in the Milky Way
counts out the Seven Sisters and tells of their origin.
He wanders over the great distances
points out moments in the star world journey.

They dance, move the air with their song
telling the stories of here –
in the shape of mountains
flight of birds, harness of rocks
secrets of water
sounds of silence.

Their stories shimmer –
beautiful as Greek starry mythology.
Olive listens to the legends –
wanders with them along the 'Yaggin road
made when the moon was human'.

5

Breakthrough 1932–1933

To our children's children
the glad tomorrow
– Oodgeroo Noonuccal

Back in Sydney

Her books, her paintings
her framed photograph of Harold
the Glebe flat, welcome Olive's return.

Images flicker across her mind –
Mick's face as he talks of his totem
stars in his eyes as he says,
'I'm a bandicoot man…'[1]
She remembers the twitch
the quiver in their ritual dance
the drum of feet hitting up red sand.
She shudders at the clank of chains
shivers at memory of young shackled wrists
chained to the court bench.
Her body softens as she remembers
the children's laughing eyes.

Through the window, leaves
illuminated by the afternoon light
tremble in the breeze.
Olive's wrath pierces the darkness.
She is driven to proclaim the truth
make people listen
understand.

Her message is a wrapped package
with a big red stamp, marked
'Urgent, act now…'
She straightens, determined to be part
of whatever unfolds.

Grog, venereal disease, a rotting frontier[2]
and a flawed justice system
demand to be addressed.
Worrying news filters in of further shootings
destruction of country.
Whispers denied, honesty compromised.

The great Australian silence.[3]
She realises many hear but turn their backs.

She stands by the window –
it frames only a small part of a darker picture.
She rages at her helplessness.
How to break down this wall of denial?

Olive inhales deeply. Her pen is her salve.

She concludes her next article in *Mankind*,
'One day it will be evident what an important part
nature – in all its forms – plays in the lives
of these appealing people – whom we have treated
and still are treating so shamefully.'[4]

Aloud into the night she hears herself wail,
'I cannot afford to hide, I will not walk away.
This is what I am called to do.'

Truth – her way

Triggered by her sense of urgency
letters and articles flow from her ink-dipped pen
to scratch of nib, dab of blotter.[5]

At Society meetings her desert experience
gives her authority. Her strong voice
fills the hall.
'It is the accepted belief, the Aboriginal people
are dying out. This is not true.
They are being killed off.'

Anger deepens her voice.
'And there is much that can be done to stop this…'[6]
Fists clenched she continues,
'…to preserve and even reanimate the lives
of these people
who have no choice…
the "full bloods" need our protection
need their own land to live their way
for they have a vital connection,
a oneness with this country.'[7]

Olive longs to tell more
of white-man law and injustice.
She sees shaking heads
raised eyebrows.
Flushed with rage she sits down.
Her words are dismissed,
too emotional, too idealistic.
Too honest!

Over supper one man advises her,
'You need to get hold of yourself.
Stop questioning.
To survive you have to be objective.
I used to think about these things,
it made me too crazy.
I now work for the government
to facilitate changes. Change is inevitable.'[8]

A battle lost

Another month, another meeting.
A grazier petitions for a land grant.
She remembers her talk with Pastor Albrecht
and of a someone wanting a lease.
She stands with fire in her eyes
names and describes this country.
'Haast's Bluff – this land is not suitable for a grant.
This place is an oasis with a sacred waterhole.
Pikilyi families are strong and healthy.'
Her hands move with urgency.
'We must demand it stay a reserve
for full-blooded Warlpiri.'[9]

Negotiations proceed, Olive is sidelined
deemed invisible.
'Yep, good plan.
Braitling will look after the people there.
It will be good for everyone
with his new leases of land –
the cattle, workers, jobs,
good for all concerned.'[10]

Olive's shoulders sag
as she listens to them
sees the shake of hands and pats on the back.
The pastoralist R.R. Braitling
is granted a lease over the Warlpiri land
and waterholes!

Her vow

Emotional, idealistic…
their barbs catch in her throat.

She dare not flinch
even as she chokes back tears
in their cigar-smoke-laden room.
Even as she moans beneath her anger
a vow of determination stirs in her.

Back at her flat, moonlight
spills silver through the window.

She pens a letter to a Tassie friend.
'Is this how the chapter reaches its end –
my theories, my pleas ignored?
Now we standby and watch
the decline, the downfall
of the innocent first people of this land.

Where does the soul of our nation lie?'[11]

Restless

In her dingy office Olive yearns
for the vast open country, large skies,
hazy horizons, a slung kettle hissing
and spitting its leak over the fire.
Burnt flesh and sizzle
of goanna still fill her nostrils.

Olive walks country in her sleep –
the pungent smell of camels
sweaty bodies, blazoned glare, flies
dust-blown storms.
That red dust under
the colour of her heart
and patter of Pitjantjatjara children
still running giggling beside her
lingers like the balm of an Indian summer.

A breakthrough

Where there is breakdown, there is often breakthrough.
– Lewis Carroll

It comes like a southerly buster
on a hot summer's day.
The new head of anthropology
at Sydney University, Raymond Firth
states in an article,
'Missionary stations sometimes tend
to destroy native culture
making Aborigines "hangers-on".'[12]

Olive finds in Firth a new kindred spirit.
She writes to him immediately
with many questions.

Firth replies,
'You would do well to study anthropology.
Come here to Sydney University.
Learn discipline and the scientific approach.
Acquisition of a diploma
will overcome emotionalist labels.
You could apply for research funds
to return and work inland where you left off.'[13]

A vision shines –
bright as Barrenjoey Lighthouse.
She arranges one afternoon a week
off from work to study.

Anticipation nurtures her dream
pulses like the turning beacon.

In the new year, aged forty-eight
Olive begins her study
for a Diploma of Anthropology
at Sydney University.

Heady days

Olive is energised by academia.
The scissor-cut horizon
of her desert experience
challenges like a mirage.

She seizes every chance to argue,
'The root cause is not malnutrition or disease –
They camouflage facts, treat the wrong symptoms.'
Heated discussion rises.
Angrily she fights for breath.
'Even the most ignorant know the problems –
white man's aggression, sexual abuse
fear, venereal disease, land dispossession.
We like to deride these facts.'
She flushes, her neck prickles as she continues,
'Full-bloods need their own protected country
not mission reserves.'
Her tone is strident.
'Daily handouts from stations
keep them tied to white man power.'[14]

A student offers his opinion.
'Isn't it the accepted method to distribute
rations daily?'
Her argument in response is emphatic
well researched.
But disagreement is loud –
voices shout Olive's words down.

She feels blindsided. Bumping
into things, things that cut, crush and hurt.
She is getting nowhere.
She leaves the tutorial
heart thumping against the prison of her ribs.
She writes to her friend Crowther in Tasmania
and is affirmed by his reply.
'Simply stay calm
give your thesis paper, do the exams,
maybe then you will be heard.'[15]

As she prepares her final paper,
the words
'where does the soul of our nation lie'
still pummel her thinking like a mantra.

Final paper – seminar

With her given topic –
Aboriginal Free Reserves
she has a sense of drowning.
She knows it's controversial
and her words will not be popular.

A sea of critical faces are her challenge.
When Dr Elkin joins the seminar
she is hit by a tsunami of doubt.
It swells with her ongoing anger against him.[16]
Crowther's letters with their refrain
of affirmation may not be enough.

She reminds herself to speak slowly.
She reads her paper loudly, stresses,
'…the need for areas of good and productive land
of which Aboriginal people
have exclusive occupancy and control…'
She continues,
'Without this
the people are black shells
…apathetic
dead inside.'[17]

Olive receives light applause
Professor Firth adds mild praise.
'It's a good idea, idealistic
but unattainable.'

A deluge of vitriol obliterates
her theory. One student says,
'I strongly advocate swift and sharp assimilation.'
Heads nod around the room.

Elkin's thin voice breaks in,
'There are so few Aboriginal people in Central Australia,'
(a region she knew he had not visited)
'alienating large tracts of land from development
is not feasible.'[18]
Nods continue.

Olive shakes her head.
Inland experience has humanised her story.
She will not be told how not to see.

She creeps home battered
takes days to face her peers.
For Olive, being marginalised
is not an option.
She will hold in. The course will equip her
for field work, allow her to apply for research funds
pay her for doing what she loves.
Further she is boosted by the thought
of an impending ANZAAS Congress
where she will give a paper.[19]

The ANZAAS Congress 1932

A tense week. Her paper
for the Congress is ready.

She places her notes in her portmanteau
a treasured heirloom.
'Today I will stand before many
influential people. This is my time,'
she says to herself.
'I am sure they will listen, understand.'[20]

In her mother's long mahogany mirror
legacy from their Tasmanian days
Olive sees the fine lines around her eyes.
'More than my mother had at forty-nine'
she wryly observes.
'Well, you wouldn't swap the desert trips
so sun lines it is.
No longer young but still a lot to do.'[21]

Navy serge skirt reaches to her ankles.
She brushes her thick-soled shoes
folds and ties her white long-sleeved blouse
high at the neck, dons her cream hat
gloves, black jacket.
Her hair is coming loose
beneath her hat –
it never keeps a pin in place.

She walks briskly to the podium
squares her shoulders
determined to make a good impression.

A knitting of passions

Olive faces a hall of curious people
her voice more assured
her presentation knitting her two passions –
Aboriginal welfare and native plants.

A quietness falls as she reads,
'I cannot stress how vital flora is –
nutritionally, medicinally and ritually.
How detrimental to well-being
is the restriction of freedom
to gather and hunt in country,
to perform ceremonies connected
to country that can be performed
nowhere else.'[22]

The gathering is astounded
by her courage, her expeditions
wide ranging research, plant specimens,
drawings and hand-drawn detailed maps.

Applause is warm, genuine.
Olive is delighted. She has made an impression!
Praise in a *Sydney Morning Herald* review thrills.

One man, Ted Strehlow from Hermannsburg
seethes in the shadows.
At a garden party on the final afternoon
he steps forward, introduces himself,
'Hear you were meddling at the Mission,'[23]
he says loudly.

Olive eyes this tall slightly hunched man.
She stands her ground,
'We passed through on my last trip.
I cannot agree with bans against their customs.
The people should be allowed their rituals.
and I see your Mission steals
their sacred stones and sells them.
The old men are crying
for their lost *tjurunga*.'[24]

Strehlow dons his hat, turns his back.
Olive shrugs, but aware of his power
and her vulnerability, fumbles with her neck bow.

Justice her sword

No one wants to look too closely
at what is going on, few want to look at all.

Olive is a lone voice
in the culture of denial.
Strong, determined, she hasn't learnt
the skill to pretend!

She seizes only the sword of justice
has small wins with several petitions –
one using her words going to the Governor
from the ANZAAS conference.

Yet she writes, 'My voice is blocked,
not ignored but actually blocked.
There is a brick wall of apathy.
At the Congress, papers given
are ignored. Even the consequences
of distributing rations daily rather than weekly
is supported. How can I explain what I witness?
The dysphoria, loss of spirit of groups
living at stations. How it results in a struggling
even dying race.'[25]

The prospect of being paid
for field research keeps her going.
She will be heard.
One day she will make a difference.

6
Research and the inland
1933

'Every hill got a meaning, missus…'
– Mick Dow Dow

Resignation

How quietly the decision arrives –
no banging at the door, no chiming of bells.

It sits with Olive in her Glebe flat
teases with doubts and dread
and office talk of her much time off!
Yet reminds her too
how she has peered all winter
at the dole queue soup kitchen
below Central Station
thankful for her job.

She hears her father's voice,
'Nobody gives up a secure job.'
Another whisper crowds in.
'Road not taken, wanting wear
annoys you forever.'

With a suddenness
that is no surprise
it whispers in her ear
challenges her,
'Take annual leave
secure a last free rail pass
return inland for five weeks
complete your thesis
then trust research funds will flow
to do what you love to do.'

Resignation morphs into freedom.

Third trip inland

The train's pace into Adelaide
is a slow rhythmic chug.
Vehicles wait at crossings
bells ring her through.

In a tunnel she catches her reflection.
The happy glimpse of a smile
startles her.
She straightens her long skirt, puts on her jacket.

Using the next flash of a tunnel
she adjusts pins
tucks her hair under her hat.

She feels a butterfly buzz.
'The gateway to the north does this to me,'
she later writes to her friend Crowther.
'Three days and I'm on the Ghan.
Horrie Simpson will meet me at Edwards Creek
for a few days of sketching,
Mick Dow Dow at Alice for the research.
All has been arranged.'[1]

Soothing stiffness from the journey
Olive rolls her shoulders.
In Adelaide, Professor Cleland meets her.
In his grey suit and tie
he looks the gentleman.
He takes off his hat and bows.
His friendly demeanour
and welcoming eyes put her at ease.

She needs him as a trusted advisor
and is forever grateful to Crowther
for connecting them.
Correspondence forges a new friendship.

She writes her appreciation.
'I feel very welcome –
especially dining with the professor and his wife
at his home.'[2]

Cleland settles Olive at the Botanic Hotel.
She smiles at the name. How oddly appropriate.
At the Museum, he and colleagues[3]
wait excitedly to show her the film
of their inland expedition.
She feels included, confident –
colleagues in unison.

They advise and assist her preparation
for the five-week journey north.

High hopes

Over dinner her enthusiasm bubbles.
'After my thesis I plan
a full year of research among the Arrernte'
she confidently tells the Professor
and others grouped around the table.
'I would like to be included
in your next museum expedition.
It will reduce my research expenses
and my anthropology will enhance the group.'[4]

Silence.

Unease rolls around the room
as lightening awaits a clap of thunder.
Awkward shifts and exchanged glances
the embarrassed clearing of throats.

From her left in a deep tone,
'That would not be possible…'

'But you took Ted Strehlow on your trip last year!'

'…for a woman,' mumbles the professor.

Exposed, Olive's heart races.
She hopes they don't notice the burn
of her cheeks.
She avoids eye contact
gazes out as one with miles to go
restless to be on her way.
She needs desert air.

'Why does gender cause such heartbreak?'
she broods into the night.
'Why wasn't I born a man!'

Tight time frame

No one meets her at Alice.
Was her letter to Mick Dow Dow
mislaid? Lost? Intercepted?
On enquiry she learns Ted Strehlow
has left a week earlier
into her planned research area.
Worse, he has taken Mick and the camels.[5]

Olive sets her jaw.
She has no time to waste.
In five weeks her rail pass finishes.
She'll act within what constrains her.

Fury drives her to action.
She wipes her sweaty brow
tucks up her hair, strides out
takes a cheap back room
in Annie Meyers' boarding house.

This blatant marginalisation
gnaws at her gut.
She sits at the kitchen table
stares morosely into space.
She has never felt so stymied.

At sunset Annie makes a cup of tea.
They sit together. Olive muses,
'I feel so alone, Annie. More than that
I am uncertain – an ache
that causes me great anguish.'

A terrible mistake?

Every cell in her body recoils
like the touch of hot coals.
Has she made a terrible mistake?
Are her dreams about to slip away?

It was a gamble to leave her secure job.
She has five weeks to complete
her quest for research grants.
For now, her own money invested
in rations and supplies.

At the post office
she puts out word for a guide.
The wait is interminable –
minutes stretch into hours
in a suffocating day.
She hears her father whisper
one of his maxims,
'And for those who patiently wait
life is fruitful.' She smiles.

With the blessing of an evening breeze
two of Mick's brothers, Jim and Charlie[6]
turn up, leading Skipper an old pack camel.
Jim smiles a warm dark glow
as he checks the camel's hooves.
'Word spreads on the wind in our country
Missus…Miss Pink, we'll take you.
We'll set out at first light
catch Mick on his way back.'

The leaves of the river red gums
shimmer in the golden dawn light
clapping hands for her journey.
As they set out, word comes from Mick.
He will meet them.

When Mick and his family find their track
Olive greets them with relief –
her bandicoot man, one whom she trusts.
He will give credibility to her research.
Mick is breathless and tired.
He looks frail and much older
yet his eyes still fire with life.

Ilpalentye Country[7]

1.

In a wide land backed
by bony slopes of rock
they become an unlikely research team.
Miss Pink stands out in long dark skirt
high white collar and fly helmet.
Mick with tied-back grey hair,
shining, scarified skin, and a contented hum.
His bearing defies his age.
With his wife Rose and their families
they trek the Two Women Dreaming Track[8]
to a white limestone ridge
where Mick sits down. He explains,
'The dreaming here belongs to my mother,
Akeye Dreaming, connected to the bush currant.'[9]

Mick sends the group ahead
to unload, prepare the tents and fires.
He leads Olive to special totem sites
and with his permission
she photographs, sketches, takes notes.

Rose binds soft branches for their beds
and shares rations for the meal –
eggs, damper and honey.

Later, Olive enjoys the solitude
of her own camp area.

With the last glint of sunlight
cool air seeps in. In the silence
she sits before a grand altar of stars
soaks up the sky, her mind and fingers
dance to the theme of her thesis.

For two weeks Olive moves
to Mick's rhythm. His stories captivate her.
'Every hill got a meaning, missus…'
His ways of moiety, totems and rituals
stretch her mind in ever widening circles.
What began as a radical choice
melds into passion.

Each day they travel to the next waterhole.
Only once do they have to double back.
Mick had yelled in disbelief,
'The waterhole is dry, someone's blasted it
to make it bigger,
broken the skin…'[10]
His words strike Olive like a lightning bolt.
She catches up, looks down in dismay
shudders with anger.
They turn back to the previous camp
and within its safety devise a new route.

2.

Like Olive, Mick wants to learn,
share and engage –
a mutual understanding.
Each new dance, ritual, story, awakens
in widening circles
deep forgotten knowings.

His sculptured body
gleams as if the light beams
from inside him.
He stands tall, his backbone the land.
This is his sense of place
belonging is his lifeline.
She senses it, feels it.
Cut off from this country
he would be severed from his source.

Olive discerns her métier –
to listen, observe, document.

Under the milky bowl of sky
by the crackle of fire where
embers spark as logs shift
Olive feels circled by time
into the deep of now
as time cycles with the moon.

With pen and ink and notebook
she ponders, chooses her words
writes of story, song and dance
of ancestors, hills, plants, trees
of stones speaking, caves singing.
'How to capture this magic…
I must write without conceit.
I must write with wonder.
Help people to see
this is liberation for us all.'[11]

The corkwood tree

Olive realises Strehlow has instructed
Mick to conceal some rituals.
This further betrayal, tears Olive apart.
To hide her fury is an enduring struggle.

Mick, also torn, works to make amends.
He shows her ground paintings
tells her more of his totems –
the bandicoot and the corkwood tree
come to life.

He declares Olive the elder sister
of the corkwood tree,
her name written Untyeye Yampa
the sweet drink of hakea nectar
and gives her a sacred *tjurunga*.

Olive stands tall with a new pride
honoured alongside his wife and mother.

She loves the hakea.
The honeyeaters dangling like acrobats
and the vital hum of bees invigorate her.
She leans against its trunk, a touch
that helps her understand the honour.

Bright star

Olive's last evening arrives.
She joins Mick and his wife
by their fire in the pink-orange
afterglow of day.
A chorus of birdsong sings away
the dying light. Her world is clear
redeemed and beautiful.

A grand stream of stars
fills her with wonder.
'Bright star,
would I were steadfast as thou art –'[12]
she murmurs under her breath.
'This life is meant for me.
I want to return and be here.'

Each day has brought sights and secrets
that delight.
She finds herself inside the dreaming
Untyeye Yampa[13]
bright as the yellow corkwood flower.

Reflection

It is time to return to Sydney.
A duchenne smile plays on Olive's face –
sorrow at leaving, joy of having been.
From the Ghan, she takes
a lingering look at country
with steadfast eyes.

In the train window she sees herself
huddled in her seat, her face
glum in a pall of dust and smoky haze.
She murmurs to her reflection
'I will speak and write
of these vulnerable people,
of this fragile land.'

Later she writes to Crowther
to tell how deeply grateful she was.
'As I paid Charlie and Mick Dow Dow
at the railway station…I said goodbye.
They raised their hats to me with great style.
They had been so splendid on the trip
… I am sorry to leave my old guide (Mick)[14]
Now it is urgent. I will write this thesis
and return here for paid research.
I want to make our country aware…
I want to make a difference.'

Whisperings from Caledon Bay[15]

There is a thread in hearts
called hope. Though it may weaken
with elusive webs of gossamer
its dark net threads through us
as warp and weft renders it
everlasting.

This day its threads are strong as twine
a crosswise weave on the loom of hearts.
It comes in the sound of voices –
a patchwork of voices speaking up.
Outrage will not be silenced
its crescendo spurred
by a breaking headline:
'Government prepares a Punitive Expedition
against Blacks – ministers, governors
and police prepare action following
the fatal spearing of a policeman.'[16]

The term punitive is stripped of ambiguity.[17]
Euphemism and sinister intentions are called out.
This time a new sensibility
will not be silent.
The Australian people pick up the thread.
They bombard the papers and radio
strongly oppose any such action
call for a better way. News spins out
into headlines around the world.[18]

On a crow-black evening
Olive sits in a dark corner of her Sydney flat
candle guttering, and does what she does best –
writes to the powers at play –
demands just action.

Behind a wall of murmurings,
the government boat *Maroubra*,
readies to carry the avengers.[19]
Her agitation increases.
Letters are not enough.

Olive walks to the Glebe Post Office
sends a telegram to Prime Minister Lyons.
'In the name of Australia
and for the sake of ordinary humanity
I plead against any decision
to send an expedition into Arnhem Land.'[20]

She is proud of her colleagues
Professor Elkin and W.E.H. (Ted) Stanner
who also strengthen the thread of hope
with letters and demands.[21]

An embarrassing telegram arrives
from the High Commissioner of Great Britain
demanding an explanation.[22]
Prime Minister Lyons denies any such plan.
He orders any expedition be stopped.
Conciliatory measures only to be taken.
A new mantle is being woven.

Olive calls it hope for the country –
the unbroken thread
weaving into hearts of people black and white
to find a way to live together in peace.[23]

7

An anthropologist
1934

We cannot live in the past but the past lives in us
– Charles Perkins

Struggle to freedom

Olive struggles with her thesis.
At Sydney University, Professor Elkin
supervises in his autocratic way
argues for tight academic process.
Her artist's eye and intuitive mind
seek the essence.

Yet only with her thesis complete
and a research grant secured
will she have the freedom she craves.
She writes and rewrites.
Frustrated she storms into her supervisor.
'It's all so colourless.
How can I show totemism?
It is an invisible force, glue of their society
their oneness with the land
like breath…that sustains life.'[1]

Words shuttle back and forth
like a ball played by the wind.
Elkin makes the catch –
finds a compromise.
'You complete the academic paper,
your thesis,' he emphasises,
'then a separate essay
can cover your personal views!'[2]

Her thesis is accepted.
Her horizon expands
as anticipation rushes through her.
A return to the inland is assured.

Diploma and research grant

A research grant fires her sense of self.
Her voice will be heard.
She looks out at Sydney Harbour
through thatched branches.
Nearby, seagulls squark.
She knows she will not miss the city.

Her mind looks inland
keen for her research year
among the Warlpiri people
with whom she shares
mutual respect

Olive can smell red dust
taste arid air, feel its stickiness on her skin
see the sunsets and big skies
anticipating her new status –
an anthropologist.

She envisages full-blood Aborigines
having land solely for their own use.
Hope might be a feather on this wind
that blows ruination.
It might prove to be wildly stubborn
but now armed
with her diploma and grant[3]
Olive savours the future.

A fourth journey inland

Bustle of porters, huff of steam
blurt of whistle, Olive revels
with this connection to country.

With notepaper and her new fountain pen
she writes to Crowther,
'It is a great achievement but it will be a tight year.
I have a research grant of £300 – it has rigorous demands.
It cuts me short with every expense –
camping equipment, food, medical supplies
reference books, collecting material, camera
notebooks –
yet my excitement is palpable.'[4]

Friends in Adelaide meet the train,
buzz about to assist her preparations.
She stops a few weeks at Alice Springs.
Annie Meyers' guest house, a familiar base
bustles with plans for her expedition.

Research expedition

1. Preparation

Olive knows her strengths
yet finances and 'privacy' wrangle.
Some of her private letters fall open.[5]
Telegrams give rise to gossip.
Ted Strehlow hovers
a raptor over his territory.

Mick Dow Dow, sends a message:
'I want to be your guide to Pikilyi but
my boss, Mr Kramer, refuses to release me.'
Olive grits her teeth, makes tea
plans her attack.

She is angry the Kramers know her plans –
'bush telegraph' keeping Strehlow informed.

Hoping to appease, Mick urges,
'Missus, Ned Ampetyane is in town.
He is a good guide
from west of the Arrernte lands…
speaks some English.'[6]

Ned turns up, small, dark
wiry and bright-eyed
with tightly curled black hair.
Olive is reassured. Her plans proceed.

Paddy Tucker and his wife Topsy
(returned from the Lasseter search)
with three riding camels and six pack camels
are also eager to work for her.
Olive is confident.
Knows she negotiates fairly
with the desert people
and is keen to set out.

2. Journey

Before dawn on a late spring morning
her entourage leaves Alice Springs.
Olive has nervously acquired an old ute
Ned's cousin Campbell is driving her.
More tribesmen with their families
have joined Olive's payroll.
Camels are laden with supplies.

Her own expedition!
Her vision a reality.[7]

They trek north-west into the Granites.
Each evening in camp she writes.
At dawn she walks and sketches.

On the fourth day near Coniston Station
she calls a halt, her voice sharp with anger.
'I will not drive past that place!
I would rather walk through a spinifex desert
than see the face of Randall Stafford.'[8]
She detours on foot
on trackless land
in stinking midday heat
collapses back into the dusty truck
dehydrated but pleased at her protest.

They arrive at Doreen Station
home of William Braitling
who now 'owns' the permanent waterhole
that Olive fought to protect.
His wife Doreen and Olive talk.
'We will give you a few extra men
to track your journey.
The going is tough from here on.'[9]

The last sixty miles
is slow going – a leaking radiator (plugged
with Olive's Cashmere Bouquet soap)
punctures, oil leak, bogs, sand slips –
they arrive exhausted at Yunmaji Waterhole
a spring sheltered by an ochre-red gorge.

Yunmaji Waterhole

Olive has truly arrived.
Her workroom is a bough shelter.
Her washroom, privy and tent
are set in the shade of three ghost gums.
Their roots burrow deeply into the sand
defy the relentless red desert.

The air smells of dried earth and eucalypt.
She looks up into a stretch of tresses
that fans minute breaths of moving air
and leans her back onto a white trunk –
a favourite tree, ever cool to the touch.
She gazes into dusk, soaks up the colours
watches flashes of blue and yellow as
butterflies hover around the waterhole.

Olive writes,
'Hundreds of small zebra finches
and crested pigeons
come in like clockwork at dusk
to quench their thirst.
The call of frogs
takes up where the birdsong leaves off.'[10]

Ned builds a smoky signal fire
to invite the Warlpiri people.
Eighteen locals walk in, set up camp.

One man has the proud bearing of an elder.
In her Edwardian long beige dress
her greying hair pulled into a twenties bun
Olive stands, reaches out her hand in welcome.

His fine strong body, greased with goanna fat
glistens with rubbings of red ochre.
With hand gestures and in language,
'My name is Nullargi, this is my wife,
and our medicine man. We make camp.
I give you skin name of Napaljarri.'[11]

Olive's face is wreathed in smiles
reassured her research will bear fruit.

Research with the Warlpiri tribe

Dawn's crescent flutters alight
catches the Tanami desert blood red.
From the shadow
life takes up its morning chorus.
Olive remembers Ooldea
hears the echo of Daisy Bate's wise counsel,
'a fixed routine for each day'.

So here, at Yunmaji she begins
with an early walk and sketching
using the cool hours
to collect and prepare plants.[12]
After breakfast she sets up a first aid post.
Word spreads, queues grow
for mixtures of her remedies
and healing from the medicine man.

Notepad in hand Olive walks
with the women and children.
She records Warlpiri words and equivalents[13]
in Arrernte. Learns more of the plants.
Together they gather grass seeds
tiny plums, the munyeroo plant
bush currants, wild honey.

Listening

Her 'cooee' calls the men up from their camps.
'Now my day's work really begins.'
Olive sits on a tea chest under a bough shelter.
Men and boys form a circle
their black oiled bodies catch the light.
She questions, listens, strives to grasp
their almost intangible kinship system.

An opus of experience

As days pass Olive detects a build of trust.
Chatter rises, sharing deepens.
Huddle of elders reach a decision.
'Missus, our aunties say we are to dance
some rituals, secrets, taboo for women
for you to write, so they are remembered.'

Her notes garner an opus of experience.
After a few weeks Nullargi
and some of the men lead her
to another sacred place
for a Kangaroo Ancestor Dance.

Confidently Olive writes,
'I am having valuable breakthroughs
and this place is out of Strehlow's reach.
Today I was given a sacred object
with a promise to keep secret the rituals.
I feel greatly moved by their trust.'[14]

Yet Ned, her interpreter, is faltering
unfocused, vague words
in an agitated mumble
his eyes often averted.
Sometimes she thinks it would be
better without him!

Truth evades

After some weeks, Ned comes to her camp.
'Missus, they quarrel over the shares of food,'
he gestures,
many are leaving the camp.
Nullargi walks in, points and shouts
with loud grumbles in language.
Ned turns his back and flees.
Olive frowns, peers with frustrated eyes.
She is helpless to understand.
Something is not right.
Nullagi returns with a new story.
'Ned has lied. He sleeps with my wife,
outside the custom, totems.'
Then the word 'boss'.
Olive tenses –
'Braitling from the station…sleeping
with the tribal women!'

Olive gasps, takes a step back
goes to her tent, heart racing
closes the flap, finds her medicine.

When Nullagi calls out he is leaving
she straightens her skirt
stands outside the tent.
Olive wrings her hands
as bitter words flood her thoughts.

'Just when I have worked so hard
and think all is going well –
all the time spent to build trust!
An exodus from the camp.
This is the end of my research!'[15]

She storms over to Braitling's post
fronts him angrily
'My research cannot go on…
people are leaving.
I have worked my guts out to get their trust.'

Braitling squirms
offers to make amends.
He calls some old men over.
Munyani, with bare feet, short shorts
and a tattered lumber jacket
comes forward.

He has a proud stature
and long curly hair reddish-grey,
tied with a white headband.
He nods his head, bows,
beckons his Pikilyi families.
She sees in his fine old face and stance –
a leader.
Near him stands Muyu
called medicine man.
Braitling grins, points to the men.

'My elixir, I give you an elder
and a renowned healer,'
he boasts, 'to assist in your research.'[16]

They meet. A new circle.
Their voices and insights fresh.
Olive writes,
'They are honest, there is no hesitation.
They want to help me know their story.'[17]

She walks country with them
listens, writes and when they dance,
'Their bodies alive
glisten with ochre,
they have a new freedom.'
Olive records,
'From under their feet the dust flies
the hills sway to the rhythm of the moon,
to seasons, in turns of light and dark
all as one, one as all with the earth.'[18]

There is rejuvenation.

8
Wings of fire
Summer 1934

A whispered fear

December howls with gritted wind
and heavy louring skies. Rain closes in.
Dysentery, a silent fear
shadows Olive.
All week she drinks brandy
with extra lemon barley water.
A careful established routine –
potassium permanganate and charcoal
to treat her drinking water.

This night, streaks of lightning flash
and catch fleeting glimpses of Olive
on her camp stretcher, feverish
cramped
spent.

At dawn she calls for Muyu.
A week of his plant medicine fails.
Many fear they will lose her.
She is unable to walk.
The camels hover nearby untethered
but Olive is too weak
for them to be of use.

The rescue

Olive drifts in and out of delirium
heat shrivels her body.
Munyani fans her with a hakea branch
to stir the stifling air.
Paddy arrives (as planned)
with fresh camels to take Olive
to the next camp.
Seeing her, he panics
sets out for help.

Braitling arrives leading a pack horse –
the car unable to get through.
Ned follows. Desperate. Their final option –
carry her out on a litter.

Braitling brews Bengers's Liquid Food
over the campfire, coaxes her to sip
to strengthen her for the journey.
Paddy helps lash her camp stretcher
to shafts of sapling with makeshift handles.
A group of Aborigines volunteer
to carry Olive through the bush.
Packhorses and camels follow
carrying her stores and gear.

Twenty-three miles of rough country.
Searing summer heat –
the bearers vary in height and strength
slip and stumble but despite ache
of shoulders and exhaustion
there is care and generosity of spirit.

At his station, Braitling's wife, Doreen
nurses Olive with fluids, lime juice
eggnogs and rest to gain strength
for the next leg of the trip.

At last the road becomes passable
Ned and Bill Braitling help her into the car
and tackle the bull dust and sand into Alice.

Life-threatening journey

It was a rough and exhausting trip.
As Ned put it, 'a matter of life and death'.
Braitling boasted later,
of his worry for Miss Pink
when crossing boggy creeks
and detouring off impossible roads!

Soon they could telegraph news
of the emergency
to the Inland Mission Hostel.
A doctor and nurse stabilise Olive
and assist her into town.

Olive starts the slow climb out
of that black hole.
Hides her face
beneath the sheet, unable to meet
the nurses' eyes, refusing to speak
to her rescuers.
Flimsy hospital clothing distresses her.
'What people must be saying?'

Out of hospital, she returns
to Annie Meyers' guesthouse.
Little by little her strength revives.
She struggles to Annie's kitchen table
sorts her papers. Writes an article
on Land Ownership
and sends it off to Pastor Elkin.

Under menacing cloud

Olive dons her long skirt, high-neck blouse
jacket and helmet fly-net.
Mick sees how she craves to be away
from prying eyes, sets her up outside town
at Painta Springs. Olive stares in dismay.

A deserted cattle camp in the dusty
and extreme March heat. With heavy rain
dry dust becomes a morass of mud.
Mick, unwell, returns to Alice Springs.
and Olive is alone on her fiftieth birthday.
Her project doomed.

A pulse of what next? What next?
burrs her dreams.

A few days later an answer comes.
A young Warlpiri man rides out
with her mail. He cuts wood
tightens the tent pegs, pumps water.

A hue of hope shines
in her hands – the journal *Oceania*.
Her report 'Land Ownership'
from her Warlpiri experience
pleases Professor Elkin. It is published.[1]
He promises a renewed grant
for further research.
Mild autumn days arrive.

Mick and his brothers return,
with a pitchi of fresh food
and lots of gossip –
'There is talk about your presence…
Pastor Strehlow warns against you.'[2]

Mick's tired eyes reassure her
'We will take you to a good place
for your research.'
They move Olive, her stores and camp
in their truck, to Junction Waterhole.
But under lowering clouds of paranoia
Olive broods on the menace
of Strehlow's presence.

Junction Waterhole

Mick and his brothers set up her tent
shaded by a stand of mulga.
She hears the gurgle of a small stream.
Positions her writing table to catch
a glimpse of Mount Gillen.
Nearby a walking track runs along the Todd.
A good site to meet people
some will remain awhile.
Healthy and strong again she details
a wealth of Arrernte customs.

Mick beams as Olive records his stories.
He reminds her of the hakea flower ritual
he shared with her last time.
'Missus, quickly write up our story of the secret
ground painting about the hakea flower
and bandicoot ancestors of Ilpalentye.'
Mick enthuses
'You will be the first, missus.'

The women-elders visit often.
She perceives their trusting eyes
listens to their narratives.
They press the younger ones to speak
aware of an urgency to draw Europeans
into a kinder understanding of their ways.
Maybe this will help preserve their culture.

Olive writes,
'No words will convey the sensibility
these women embody. They imbue a wisdom
I do not have words for.' She continues,
'The evening is blissful under a starry sky.
There are songs and dances for everything.
As we grapple with understanding of kinship
we still cannot know
how it works in ceremonial life.'[3]

During evenings, as the fire dies to embers
she writes by her dim kerosene lamp.
She realises there is more openness
with out-station men not caught in Strehlow's web.
Letters of complaint about
Strehlow's influence do Olive no favours
with the powers down south.

Wings afire

A telegram arrives from Professor Elkin –
confirming a further research grant.
Olive forsakes security, health, reputation
to take a new expedition further north
with the less charted Warlpiri people.
Her wings afire, she feels
a new sense of freedom
away from the oppression of Strehlow.

Bob, Mick's cousin, a well respected elder
living at the Telegraph Station
is honoured to be her guide.
A deal is sealed over tea and scones.

With revised plans, an unlikely crew
sets out north then west.
Bob six feet tall, his long beard
gives a reassuring touch
and Jack Peltharre a proud old man
small, wily with a mop of tousled grey hair
their families and Olive.
Olive in jodhpurs, boots, white long-sleeve
blouse with high necked Edwardian tie,
pith helmet and fly net.

At Chilla Well they set up first camp
by the Tanami's Jila soakage. Smoke
from their night fire signals their presence.
Munyani, the Warlpiri elder, reappears.

Olive, with renewed vigour, smiles a welcome
and uses her expanding language skills.
Bob and Peltharre translate for her.
'They will come for two moons.
You will help feed them.
They will make camp with their families.
They will hunt for meat
and will walk with you each day
and show you around their country.'[4]

She climbs the hill and waits.
At dusk, just as agreed
elders Munyani, Japaljarri and families
walk from the tea tree scrub –
men and youths carry shields
boomerangs, spears and woomeras
women and children, and a baby
snug in a bark coolamon.
They build her a strong humpy
from branches and grasses.

Each dusk the women gather food
and at a large well grooved rock
grind grass seed with a small round stone
add water, roll into cakes of dark paste
then cook them in the hot ashes.
Olive's eyes glow with curiosity and pleasure.

Children run to her with flowers.
She sketches the plants
learns their Warlpiri words
records their culinary and medicinal uses.
Aeroplanes appear in the sky.
'Noisy birds, don't be afraid,' she assures them.[5]

Her notes grow, a jigsaw of knowledge.

She comments in a letter to Crowther,
'My notes look like a complicated painting,
every stroke, every streak-line is challenging.
I want to put it in order, draw it together.
It jumps about like a happy frog in a billabong,
and sings a song of a whipamaloo.'[6]

At the end of her research
her departure is summed up by Japaljarri.
'I will not return to this camp
until your tracks have disappeared.
The sight of them will make me too sad.'[7]

9
The quest
1935–1938

Secular sanctuary

Back in the bustle of Sydney
the fetid air weighs Olive down.
The rumble and clash of argument
about inland politics is taxing
and sculpts her resolve
to work once more with the Warlpiri.

Olive seeks a renewed grant.
Her vision for full-blood Aborigines
expands into a 'secular sanctuary'[1]
protected from outside influence –
not run by missionaries
nor interfered with by pastoralists or miners
nor dictated by governments.

There are hurdles to jump –
research to be written
submitted for publication
papers to give.
Olive must lobby for this vision.

SOS Alarm

Olive narrows her quest –
to save one group
her Warlpiri full-blood Aborigines
still living on their country.

She writes a letter to Professor Elkin[2]
scratchy but resolute. Its large printing,
underlining, multiple exclamation marks
red arrows and PS notes in the margin
demand attention.

'This is urgent,' she writes.
'A secular reserve is needed.
A secular sanctuary closed to prospectors.'[3]

Mining close by intensifies her fear
for the word gold
brings fever to cool minds.
Already she hears the ploy –
'fifty unemployed men sent for mining'
and blanches at Braitling's plans
for a stock route across the land.

Support for her quest is subdued
and to her annoyance, often muted
yet she knows there are other voices who hear her.
She is not alone.[4]

Melbourne Congress

Olive writes letters to politicians
heads of government, newspapers
lifting the lid from the steaming pressure
of her resolve.
Her anxiety quietens to a simmer.

With her sights on ANZAAS, she arrives
in Melbourne over-weary
but with two papers prepared
and plans to lobby for the Warlpiri Reserve.[5]

She stands before her colleagues
and the wider community of scientists.
Not only is her experience on the line
but her reputation as a scholar.

'Cultural Contact among the Australian Aborigines,'[6]
she reads loudly
glances at the audience
knowing even the title annoys some.
She catches Strehlow's distain
fury on Elkin's face.

Afterwards…the garden party –
cucumber finger sandwiches, petit fours
served in a battle field of murmurings.
If looks were bullets
Olive would be on the ground.
She scoops red fruity punch into a glass
grateful for Cleland's reserved support
and some smatterings of praise.
Frosty nods sap her resolve.

She reads her second paper
'Land Ownership among the Arrernte'.
The room is silenced by her vocal attacks
against pastoralists and missionaries.

Olive walks tall, holds their gaze
but such armour is not enough
to shield her from the pastoralist Braitling.
Her words threaten his land.
'You plan a human zoo,' he sledges.
She lurches as if she has been punched.
Worse is to come.

He attacks her qualifications[7]
attempts to destroy her reputation.
The blows fall swiftly –
as he blames her for holding up development
paints her as inept and troublesome[8]
weak and unable to handle rough conditions.

Olive takes solace on the train back to Sydney.
Her one triumph – she secured the numbers
to support her 'sanctuary' petition.
Now endorsed by ANZAAS
it will go to the Governor.

Camouflage

Olive seeks refuge in her Glebe flat
yet as a sunflower opens
to be picked clean by crows
Olive opens herself to risk
speaking out at every opportunity
even if it means ridicule.
This year she insists her name
be on the lecture program
of Sydney's Anthropological Society.
She is a founding member
who will no longer be sidelined.

A series of essays to explore the theme
'camouflage' is her task.
Later she notes,
'I wrote these essays with my heart's blood
knowing how vulnerable
to criticism they would make me.'

The night of the Society lecture arrives
miserable and cold –
only fifteen people attend
some antagonistic to her theories.

She strides to the podium
shows a Lewis Carroll sketch
and adds,
'We weep behind our pocket handkerchiefs
where Australian Aborigines are concerned,
while we take from them with the other hand.'[9]

She looks directly out at the gathering.
'The truth in Central Australia is camouflaged.
Processes of missionaries, government policies
work of anthropologists, all camouflage
their spirit.'
She makes a case for the many wrenched away
'taught to be "sham" Christians –
for many just Aboriginal "shells"
with no remaining cultural identity.'[10]

A thunderbolt galvanises academic circles.
A letter from the ANRC accuses her of disloyalty.
Olive muses,
'I expected real scientists to accept criticism
and opposing views, in a calm and measured way.'[11]

Hobnail boots

1935. Olive's only brother and his wife
drown in a boating accident
leaving three adult daughters
and only frugal income.
Olive is devastated.
She wallows in quicksand
as she searches for consoling words.

A paltry new grant comes through –
half what the men get
and to be given monthly.
Not enough to complete her Warlpiri research.

She writes in a letter to her friend Violet,
'I feel as if a giant with hobnail boots
is treading on me.
All in all a hateful year.'[12]

Back in Alice Springs

Yet the lure of the desert
with hope of the 'future sanctuary'
is too much to resist.
Back in Alice Springs
Olive has a sense of coming home.

Stretching her grant to the limit
she invites Jim and Jack Peltharre
to be her guides as once again
she heads up the Tanami.
From her tent she walks each day
creates a narrative
linked to the dreaming tracks
marked on maps she is compiling.

Then comes a public telegram of 'recall.'
She is numb, embarrassed –
falters under a scornful gaze.
'What do the locals know?'
These words mockingly play on her mind
the guillotine has dropped –
'Your grant is not continued'!

Purpose with passion

Olive refuses to be driven
from the field.[13]
Agreed pay with her guides
must be honoured.
Loyalty must be requited.
She uses her personal savings
to complete her work
and in her own time.

She is confronted
by a system of male domination –
a barren mountain within anthropology.
She writes, 'A clutch of ageing knights
hold the purse strings for grants.'

Even Cleland is silent.
She fumes as she writes him a letter
angry at his 'collusion' with Strehlow.
Beneath her anger she also knows
she needs him
as advisor politically and personally.[14]

Is it the end?

Her resources expended, Olive packs.
Her trusted friend Stormy Campbell[15]
drives the old chevy to pick her up.
At Aileron, eighty miles north of Alice
she takes a room at the pub,
cheap and close to elders.
She begins to write up her notes.

Heat and humidity intensify her heart condition.
'My hand does not connect with my mind
in this bawdy drinking culture, rough noise,
and crude whistling whenever I appear.'
Olive returns to Alice Springs
and rents Annie's cheapest back room.
to write up her notes and wonders
'How can this work out?'

Crowther offers to lend her a house
back in her home town of Hobart.
'Come back. You will be invaluable
in ethnography at our museum.
You have friends here.'[16]

In humid heavy air the rains fall.
The Todd River floods
roads impassable, the races cancelled
and Olive is marooned.

Her old defiance tightens in her chest.
Her distress letters to Elkin produce
a small extra grant with a note,
'for your unfair treatment while I was overseas!'[17]

Olive is stunned.
Dark thoughts rush in
weary from sleepless nights at the pub
her rage, suppressed for so long, roils.
She reads his words over and over.
'Elkin admits I have been badly treated.
What am I to make of this?'

She makes a morning cup of tea
and sits with Annie –
pink dressing gown and slippers
fortification against the world.
Olive pours their tea and blurts out,
'Annie, I feel beaten.'

She taps her fingers on her cup
continues in a half whisper,
'I am humiliated by the telegrams
refusing me a grant, recalling me from the field.
People in town are talking about me,
They know all my business –
I hear them laughing as I pass.'[18]

In the long silence, they sip their tea.
Olive nibbles on a milk arrowroot biscuit.
'They made up that story
of my health and safety at risk.'

Her brow wrinkles with a familiar frown.
'I was making progress.
The Warlpiri women cared for me.
I love the children. Now I have let them down.
The men were sharing. I had their trust.
They have gone. I could keep them no longer.'
She pours a second cup of tea and adds,
'Professor Elkin says Ted Strehlow
was behind my dismissal.'[19]

Sitting on the veranda, Olive puts down her cup
shakes her head in disgust, sighs deeply.
'I cannot fight them. There is no support.
Elkin dismisses my anger –
says there is no use worrying about it.'[20]

Annie nods sympathetically.
Olive's mind is made up.
She will return to Tasmania.

Back to Hobart

A convoy of seagulls squawk a welcome
escort Olive's ship into the harbour.[21]
Up on deck Olive tastes the chill
of her homeland.

Mt Kunanyi in a mantilla of autumn mist
holds its eerie mystery.
Olive sets herself up in a small cottage
in its foothills.
On her walks, flashes of memory
bring images with colour and sound –
often she senses her father, sometimes
hears his voice amongst the brittle
crunch of leaves underfoot
pictures him crouched down
showing her a wildflower,
naming shrubs and trees.

A fog wraps around the cottage
smudges the view from her misty window.
At the table she unravels the complexity
 of her notebooks.
Her mind spins with the task ahead.
More questions than answers.
The worry that niggles and invades her thoughts –
'how to keep faith
with the Warlpiri men who trust me?'

She writes to Elkin, consumed with indecision,
'It's over. I cannot work the way you want,
so much is given to me in trust.
I am not comfortable to share.'
He reminds her,
'You have a contract with the ANRC
which has paid for your research.
You have responsibility.
Your research is important to us.'

Fidelity

Heavy with worry and responsibility
Olive writes up her field notes.
Her mood measured by dab after dab
of blotting paper on wet ink.
While her thesis hangs over her
she writes articles for *Oceania*.

Sometimes she escapes her writing
to work at the Hobart Museum.
Crowther welcomes her, pays for her expertise.
She creates a diorama for the Museum
of the Central Australian people.[22]
Confident in advising, she is open and free
sharing information on collections.

Letters go back and forth.
Elkin angry that she is away so long.
Olive writes again,
'When one does not treat natives
as specimens for study, it is very difficult
to do justice to the data –
while not 'letting down' one's friends
who trusted me with secret material
not to be published.'[23]

His letters, requests, demands
do not sway her.
Compromise impossible.
Her mind is made up. She will not betray
the elders of the Arrernte and Warlpiri people.
This means the end of her research grants.

Olive's path is spiked with loss as fierce
as the spinifex that blocks desert tracks.
The end of her career.
The end of her dream.

A door closes

Anguish builds in her body.
She boxes and seals the writings
where trust of elders is involved –
labelled 'Not to be used'.

Olive has endured her hometown
winter flurries of ice and snow
a year of greys and greens
warmed by friends and memories.

Now armed with her manuscript
she says farewell to Kunanyi, her mountain.
The door closes on Hobart.

Up on deck the endless stretch of sea[24]
stills her panic. 'What is done is done!'
The line of the horizon draws her like rope
thrown to the drowning
the sound of waves coils around her.
In whispers of the wind
she hears her father's voice.
'Remember, there is always "just beyond".'

Sydney University. She faces Professor Elkin.
He is the icy top of Kunanyi.
He receives her in silence.

'I have this enormous sense of…of…'
she trails off
her hands make empty circles in the air
'…of trust.' He barely speaks.

Accepts her submission.
She catches the sharp edge of his anger.
Her eyes sting. She walks away.[25]

10
The world in transition
1939–1946

Return to Alice Springs

Olive is drawn back inland.
It's redder than she remembers.
Closer to orange. Like rust. Like fire.

On the veranda of the hostel
she closes her eyes
listens to the hum of desert air
so different to the echoing of Hobart
or tram rattle and sharp alley
of Sydney's clatter.

She reads and rereads a note
from the Native Protector
refusing her permission
to visit any Aboriginal community.[1]

Annie joins Olive for tea.
Even as she mourns the changes
with the road north open to Darwin,
it feels as if she's never left.

She bites hard on her lip, tastes blood.
'I don't know how I got here, Annie.'
Her voice cracks '…how my life has come to this.
I don't know where I am meant to belong…'
She takes a ragged breath, voice trailing off.

Answers come in the mail.
A generous donation from a Quaker friend
money for a truck
and Tom Wright's confirmation
of an allowance
from the Sheetmetal Workers Union Fund.[2]

Her home on Warlpiri country

Olive's fifty-six-year-old fervour
blazes in her eyes.
She will not be deterred.
With Warlpiri elders and friends
she plans her own temporary place.

She loads her green 1924 Chevrolet
with tent and supplies
and with Stormy Campbell her driver and friend
moves to Thompson's Rock Hole
along the Tanami Desert Road
on Warlpiri country.[3]
Here she awaits answer to her application –
a lease for life
of nearby Crown land
with the secure Papinya waterhole.[4]

She chooses the aegis of an old desert oak[5]
hoping its feather-duster foliage will fan the air.
Locals rally about, set up her tent –
a roof shelter of tree boughs
shade for her stretcher, an old car seat
and the Chevy as windbreak.

Warlpiri people see the smoke of her fire
stroll in, make camp.
Olive jumps to her feet
when elders offer trips onto country.

Their families gather at evening, share food
laugh lots over her stumbling attempts
at language. Olive fills notepads
the pluck of her pen, the sound of lips
opening to a smile.
She writes to her nieces,
'It is dusty and difficult to live here!
I have been trying to paint some cards…
but they are very badly painted.
It is no joke trying to do it either in the hot tent
(to get out of wind)
or in wind and heat under brush shelter
between tent and car.
So is it any wonder that they are not masterpieces.'[6]

Over the next few years she adds
a cool and shady spinifex hut
declaring,
'This is home. I am planted here,
deep as the tap root of this old oak.'[7]

World War Two

Terror of Japanese invasion
strikes at the heart of Alice.
Women and children are evacuated.

The sound of military trucks
racing up and down to Darwin
on the new North Road
heightens the urgency
for Olive's quest – 'a secular sanctuary'.[8]

Propaganda spawns mixed messages
rumours of Darwin bombings denied.[9]
Newspapers headline fear and dread
yet for Olive in 1942, her fear and dread
is for the welfare of the Aboriginal people
especially the women –
vulnerable – with increased troop movement.
She anxiously awaits reply for the lease of land
yet fractured thoughts invade Olive's sleep.

Desert living

The old men point the way.
Olive follows.
Whistling kites, red firebirds of the sky
hang on morning updrafts.
Orange grasshoppers dart from spinifex.
The shape of hills, rocks, trees
make stories in ancestral walking –
'We are the stories while the walking lasts' –
stories so deeply planted,
they jolt at the marrow. She wonders
if she really hears them at all.

They talk, draw in the red soil
point to the landscape and draw more.
They give her song and dance
fill every whim of her curiosity.
She has little time to write on the journey.
It must wait.

Back at camp Olive absorbs
bubbly glee of children's play
and women prepare a fire and tucker.
To be included is always an honour.

As the sun shifts across the sky
and shadows lengthen
she writes to her niece,
'When I lie on the stretcher in the shade of the truck,
the birds come about, dozens of crimson chats
with their scarlet breasts, all the colour of the fallen blossoms
they eat or drink from…really more vermillion.

The actual thing is wonderful.
I include a drawing of a wood swallow
on a local bean tree I think eating grubs
in the red bean blossoms.
I have to wear my fly veil constantly.
The flies are extreme
and sweat so bad my pince-nez slips.
I live on tinned food, and with what I can grow.
Kraft cheese, honey, potatoes and onions are staples
bush tucker a regular treat.
The balancing compensations are
the colours of the sky, the bird life
and walks into country with the elders.'[10]

Routine at Thompson's Rockhole

The first birds of dawn are Olive's call –
the soft light perfect for gardening
and avoiding flies.

After a splish splash splosh she dresses
walks into the quietness of day
washes out some new tins, pierces holes
prepares plants – a few more lavender seeds
staggered parsley and mint.
She transplants rosemary
from jam tin to kerosene tin
marvels as the bees caress the flowers
legs yellow with pollen.
The morning smell of eucalypt
fresh as a maiden's breath
mingles rosemary-honey
that the women and children often bring.
Thyme, marjoram and parsley
thrive in a tea box.
She picks a few flowers to decorate her meal tray
– today delicate mauve pom-poms
and yellow cowslip.
'Ah, their glorious colour
buoys me, uplifts my spirits.'

She carries a jam tin of water
to each, checks protective nets
against those who would munch.

Shy rock wallabies sit close by
stock still, watching
as if they know her.

She hears the chatter and giggles
of children first, then the women shyly arrive.
She attends to their first-aid needs
and they share a harvest walk.
They cook over the fire, brew tea
in her black billy, their presence
as one with the earth
firm under her feet.

Courage

Newspapers and supplies accompany her mail.
She reads the news of the world
of the carnage, warfare blazing
lists of dead.
'Where is there an end of it?'
She reads local news. The scant
Aboriginal references distress her.
She studies the page of court cases.
Realises nothing has changed.

New policies of school segregation[11]
sharpen a strike of discord.
There is no end of being courageous in word.
When will someone listen?
She shows no fear of being labelled Communist.
ASIO will not daunt her mettle.[12]

She opens a parcel with new bottles
of Waterman's blue-black ink.
Gall and copper smell
sharpens her anger.
She brushes the dust and sand from her makeshift
army table, her throat choked, her voice gruff.
Her breath settles like embers in the morning fire
as she writes her anger
to governments and newspapers
of the 'iron curtain being formed
by Native Affairs and missionaries'.[13]

The reality of drought bites. Wind and heat
chisel each day. Olive watches
the silent withering of her garden
as the wind wrinkles, slides and sweeps
across the land.

Birthday

Olive records dry dusty air –
her garden shrivelling
bush food scarce.

Yet it is her 60th birthday
and she turns her pen
from 'official matters of consequence'
to a light-hearted moment with her nieces.
'I don't think age is counted in years.
Some people are old at 20 (in mind)
and some at age 94 young! –
as is my beloved Tassie friend Violet.
She is tremendously interested
in modern problems and especially
in the post-war world (which she may never see)…
so now I am sixty,
don't dare call me an old lady
even if I am in body! –
or you won't be invited
to come and eat "witchery grubs" and "goannas"
on my Wailbryyabbalong Estate at Papinya –
so there!
(you probably won't want to)'[14]

Hiroshima

Newspapers outrage her.
'City lying in ashes and rubble
…the impact of the bomb was so terrific
that practically all living things,
human and animal,
were literally seared to death.
All the dead and injured
burned beyond recognition.'[15]

Olive reads every article
searching for understanding.
Evil incarnate!
She cannot find words to explain
these shameful doings.
She feels terribly isolated.
Earthy chatter around the fire, no solace.
A heavy heart weighs on her
like the broken limb of a gum.

Desert dreaming dies

As the years pass
people trickle in, trickle out.

Flow, in the 'permanent' water-soak
dwindles
Vice-like weather grips the land.
Water starved country dries to dust.
Olive has long watched the creeping
invasion of mining and cattle.
Despite her pleas the land languishes.
The people who once followed
the seasons have nowhere to go!

She writes a code red to the paper.
'Here are added reasons for a
Royal Commission,
where witnesses who are analytical realists,
and not wearers of rose-coloured glasses,
could be called.
A thorough, unhurried investigation
by a body of experts (both sexes) in a dozen fields
is required to do anything worthwhile
to change the present control
which has proved rotten to the core.'[16]

From eerie stillness to a willy-willy
a wind storm rips. Roaring
red bull dust suffocates, blinds,
smothers the hard-earned garden.
Her tent falls.
Olive clambers into the truck –
her only protection.

Days later she stands
breathes the thick air and stares
at an opal cloudless sky.
Her feet, once planted securely
shift uneasily.
'There is no promise in that sky,'
she says to one of the elders
as he returns, hands empty from the hunt.[17]

Time hangs heavy
like days before an execution.
Drought's clawing fingers
sweep in, clutch at hope.
Children wail, hollow-eyed and hungry.
Wailing gives way to sullenness.

People from the gold field
walk in ill from malnutrition
gonorrhoea, pneumonia.
Many Warlpiri adults, ribbed and weak
carry their crying children.

Summer sun sears, sucks
every drop of dew. In the stifling air
ghostly silence at the empty waterhole –
as if a spell has put the frogs and crickets
into deep sleep, while lined faces search
the brassy sky for signs of relief.
Her sanctuary dream fades.
Lease of Papinya fades
throttled by drought.

Olive does not want to return to Alice
but quickly her choices narrow.
Hunger walks hand in hand with death.
Fights erupt.
Bob, her trusted friend, arrives
with his three wives and families.
Some of the children are dying.
Olive shares her food –
her last supplies are depleted.

Olive's world collapses

Desperate times, desperate measures.
The government sets up a ration depot[18]
trucks all Indigenous people to a camp –
in a bleak corner of the country.

The Warlpiri people are taken
from their land. They are helpless.
Olive is helpless.

'You must go to the government food depot,'
Olive tells Bob and the others still with her.
'I stay to help you, missus,
then I join them.'

Olive and Bob stand in a fog of choking dust
farewell his family on the last convoy of trucks.

As the dust settles Olive gazes around.
The country is desolate, empty. She is broken.
Her Warlpiri dream has vanished.[19]

The escape to safety

'They say dreams turn to dust,'
Olive muses to Bob
still choked from the trucks' departure.
'Now I understand. This hot dry air is hell,'
she mumbles, as she wipes her eyes.

With a bird's eye view
she imagines herself
an indistinguishable dot
lost in the expanse of desert.

'We have a long trek overland
to get you to safety,' Bob says.
'I will walk with you.
We will set out before dawn.'

Once again Olive Pink walks away
from her camp
from her garden
from her dream.

Her heart murmurs uneasily
as she hovers
on the edge of malnutrition.
Their journey back to Alice Springs
on a track of rutted bull dust
threatens and exhausts them.
Deep holes and detours sap
the last of their spirit and strength.[20]

11
Living in Alice Springs
1946

A fierce campaigner

In Alice Springs some friends
help Olive set up camp on the edge of town.[1]
She emerges from her tent each day
walks for supplies and to the post office.
An eccentric but striking figure
in long skirt, high-necked blouse,
signature brown felt hat and fly veil.

'Good morning, Miss Blue!'
children poke fun, giggle, tease, run away.

On the pub veranda
men whistle, make bawdy remarks.
Olive, head down, storms past.

After four years on country
a modern Alice Springs greets Olive.
War, like the multi-armed god Shiva
is both destructive and creative –
heartache and loss for many
money and progress for others.
It brings new business
an expanded town.

'Yet where is justice in this progress,'
writes Olive to Tom Wright,
'with so many despondent in the park
the begging, the amount of alcohol
and the gaol –
full of unfortunate blacks
used as slaves for the most despicable jobs?'[2]

Strikes for wages and conditions
in the Pilbara hearten Olive.
She is always buoyed by reports
showing the people taking their own power.[3]

Olive's disgust spurs her letter writing.
She speaks out –
now a fierce political campaigner
for Aboriginal justice in town.

Home Hut

Decommissioned army huts sit empty.
Sixty-feet-long corrugated-iron
pitched roofs, unglazed windows.
Olive chooses one with remnants
of an old Afghan garden, a fig tree
citrus and vines[4]
and she names it Home Hut.

She begins anew
grows herbs and flowers.
She makes a bird bath under the fig tree
plants violets, daffodils and iris
hangs 200 watercolours and sketches
of wildflowers from her journeys
sets up a museum of artefacts,
and samples of dried arid plants.
She charges an entry fee[5]
sells her handmade cards
and calendars to tourists
grows produce for locals and hotels.

Olive entertains visitors.
Those she chooses get afternoon tea
in her white china tea set.

The artist Sidney Nolan and his wife[6]
spend 'a charming afternoon
wandering through her garden and museum
with an interesting chat about many things'.[7]

Others from the south especially students
seek out this 'experienced woman'
who welcomes them and answers their questions.
Some become life friends.

Her income is further bolstered
by a cleaning job at the court house.

The courtroom

For Olive the courthouse
is a weeping sore of injustice.
Mornings, around the dusty ground
outside the court, look like a first-aid post
in war time.
Barefoot young men – many boys –
hang around. Called inside, the accused
face a law they do not grasp
in a language they cannot understand.

The court placates
bides time, imposes penalties.

Olive mops floors, dusts benches
cleans washrooms, leaving
the courtroom door ajar, annoyed
at what she hears.
She calls out angrily, interrupts
the procedure. The magistrate demands
she leave. Sometimes she is evicted
still shouting her opinion.

To assuage her rage she sits at a bench
in the back room of the court
composes protest articles and letters.

Justice denied

In the street near the Todd
Olive meets a Warlpiri man
just released from prison.
Bruised. Eyes dulled.
'Bashed up, missus,' he groans.

Olive remembers the sunlight
that filled his eyes –
on the carefree walks around country.

Her chest tightens,
'How can I watch silently
this unjust treatment?'
Tears well up. Anger dries them.
The pound of her stride reaches
a crescendo. She bangs on the door
marked 'Magistrate'.

A wide desk separates them.
A portrait of the King hangs
over his bald head like a crown.
He sits in military uniform,
sword of authority by his side.
She struggles to hide her disgust.
'Where are the scales
to balance mercy in this office?
I have the interest and welfare
of these people at heart.
I request permission to visit the prison.'[8]

Her request is refused. She writes letter
after letter to the Governor in Darwin
and to newspapers.
Blindness remains as thick red dust
on a windowpane.

She needs to be better informed
and must have access to the gaol.
The answer is a firm NO!
Back at Home Hut she devises a plan!

A fine or prison!

The following week she seizes her opportunity.
A case against two Warlpiri men
accused of stealing cattle.

Olive stands and shouts
demanding they have an interpreter –
and refuses to leave the court.

She is arrested
accused of interrupting justice
sentenced to face court
the following week.

Standing before the bench
she states, 'I want it known
I'm contemptuous of this court.'
She refuses to be contrite
and is given a £30 fine.

With a half smile, disguised
as a disgusted frown
she refuses to pay.

Olive opts for three days in gaol.

Word quickly filters through
Miss Pink is to be gaoled.

Tappy Williams, head gaoler,
who calls her 'a nosey interferer'
jumps in his car
drives hurriedly to the courthouse

and 'generously' pays her fine.

12
Friendships
1947–1955

Generosity

Maybe it's a chance encounter
maybe he waits deliberately
at the post office.

'You are the anthropologist?' he inquires,
taking off his hat, bowing his head slightly.
Olive looks up at a fresh young face
stilled by this open recognition.

She has heard reports of the new doctor
arriving to survey Indigenous health.
He is slender, leaner than she imagined.

Doctor John Hargrave is hesitant
having heard stories about Olive
yet instant rapport shines in their eyes
a merge of innocence and wisdom.

Olive invites him for afternoon tea.
She spreads out the white china tea set
madeira cake, milk arrowroot biscuits.

The squeak of the gate into her garden
sends a quiver through her. She feels
young again, glances down at her blouse
neatens her bow.

Olive and John talk into the fading light.
Her advice on culture and tradition – invaluable.
Her generosity in giving – invaluable.
They part as kindred spirits.[1]

Visitors to Home Hut

The gate, rusting open, alerts Olive.
She looks up from her couch
near the bird bath. Lorikeets sense the change
and fly off. Olive is at home surrounded by the
'lovely old orange, lemon and fig orchard
and vineyard established by the Afghans'.[2]

Her eyes beam at the sight of Bruno Dow Dow
her old Warlpiri guide, making his way
towards her. His family trail in.
Some, lower their eyes, hang back.
He removes his hat
nods with a warm smile.
He looks so frail and small now –
caved chest, his ribs obvious.
Bruno relates the news –
that Mick, his brother has died
in his home country.
They talk about the old days.
Olive reminds him of the first time
she saw them with their camels.
Smiles of recollection, warm faces.
She remembers how their dark skin
glistened in the afternoon light
and how they offered to be her guides
for her first expedition.

She sets out afternoon tea
with plenty of biscuits.
The grandchildren gather around.
Olive, with gentle mirth, swaps
English words for Warlpiri wisdom.

After they leave, Olive sits
for a long while.
She ponders the loss of Mick
how with his passing something special
is disappearing. It adds new fuel
to her blast in letter writing
about inequality and injustice.

White Australia

Olive concerns herself with the welfare
of the Aborigines who arrive in town
and enjoys their visits.
Many white people only relate
to them as either
a charitable activity or at best, as servant.
Crossing colour boundaries is not acceptable
in this budding white Australia.
She scorns the term 'gone native'
and the divisive conventions of society
building up since the war.[3]

Amelia Kunoth, a local Aborigine
trained as a nurse, befriends Olive.
Both frail and grey haired
Amelia and Olive enjoy walks
about town, têtes-à-têtes.[4]

Olive prickles at the spectral winds
aware some folk cross the street
when they see them coming.
Faces flushed from barbs of slander
they hold their heads high.

Supportive locals are always welcome.
Olive eagerly invites friends from
Tasmania, university students
and others that interest her to visit.

She enjoys anyone who will converse
on Aboriginal welfare, politics,
plants, birds and art. She quickly
calls out closed minds, rail sitters
and those of 'frivolous chatter'.[5]

Billy Goat Hill

Olive loves evening walks along the Todd.
She follows the sounds of chatter.
A group of Warlpiri people sit around a fire
by a waterhole big enough to wash in
cooled by the overhang of river red gums.
They call out endearingly, 'Talkinjiya.'

She continues up the far bank
onto the crown land designated
'useless for cattle'.
A red dirt goat trail entices her
through low-lying spinifex, emu bushes
buffalo grass and skinny desert oaks
where clusters of mulga and crimson myrtles
hide purple and white smoke-bush flowers.

Olive smiles, aware of peering eyes –
euros, wallabies and goats.
She notes the varieties of mulga.
Finally, hot and breathless
she perches on an outcrop of rock.
Clothes cling to her skin
she mops her brow, takes a deep breath.

In a space between two stands of trees
she notices the rocks
running down to touch the bush.
She is captivated
by the bounce of the sunset
a periwinkle patchwork
cerulean, violet and unexpected
tones of rainbow colour.

In sudden panic she jumps up
alert to the impending dark.
She steadies herself, faint and lost.
With a rustle of leaves
a dark figure is glimpsed in the bush.
He parts the tangled scrub
amazed to see her –
a white woman alone on country.

A hunter! With dead wallaby
on his sturdy shoulders
its palisade of legs like sticks, point to the stars.

Olive quietens her breath.
His beaming light eyes smile.
He knows of Talkinjiya from his own country.[6]

'Missus, it is dark.
I lead you back to the Todd.
My name is Jampijinpa…Johnny.'

Albert

Olive welcomes Namatjira at the gate.[7]
He follows her down the path.

'First I will show you your paintings.
I have them all these twenty years.'
Albert and Olive stand side by side
pondering the canvases.
Olive rubs her hands as they stand together.
'There's a sense that they're alive
they talk back to me.
I can tell a man of spirit
painted these.'
Albert shakes his head.
'I can swap you for better ones.
I was just beginning then.'[8]

'No. I will never part with these.
But now you are a renowned artist
you could sign them!'
He smiles and they sit for tea.

Whenever Albert is in town
they meet over tea and cake
they converse on art and hills and trees.

Excitedly she writes to her nieces,
'Did you see that the Arunda artist Albert Namatjira
had a one-man show in Sydney and sold
£1,000-worth of paintings?
I have two. I think you would like them
so simple in expression and colour and yet so true.'[9]

A few months later she writes to Crowther,

'I do not know if I showed you two painting by Albert Namatjira that I own – when I was last in Hobart? I bought them at Hermannsburg from Albert in 1936. He was just a beginner, but a brilliant one – in his simplicity of treatment of his subject. They have a spiritual quality. I am very happy with them. He still visits me frequently in town.

And I would never exchange them for any of his later works. He signed them for me. I would like to donate them to your Museum in my will but I would like to keep them here with me while I'm alive as I love them.'[10]

Olive the Advocate

On one visit Albert's steps drag.
There is mourning in his voice.
Olive feels a stirring deep down
taps her lip lightly
listens as he explains.
'My money is withheld
tax demanded –
even though I'm not a citizen
and they offer me land
not belonging to my country.
They refuse my residency in town.'[11]
Olive's advocacy on his behalf
evaporates in the hot dust.
Policies of the day do not cope
with an Aborigine being a household name.

When he is gaoled for sharing alcohol
Olive writes urgently
to the Administrator
accusing them of hypocrisy.
'He breaks no law of his own wild clan
which says, "Share all with your fellow-man."'

Olive sends a telegram to Minister Hasluck.
'Please be sure to read at once, my letter,
registered airmail, arriving Friday fifth.'[12]

Albert languished in jail for six months.
Later, Hasluck apologised for his tardiness.

A few months after his release
word comes that Albert Namatjira
has died at fifty-four.
Olive grieved.
Most Australians grieved
some shocked at what Australia had done.[13]

Bruno Dow Dow

Dragging footsteps bring disturbing news.
Two grandchildren of her first guide Bruno
come to her hut empty-handed.
Their grandfather, the elder
who cared for her, taught her so much
is too weak to walk to town.

Olive is refused a visiting permit
to visit her friend at the reserve.
She is deemed 'a trouble-maker'
suspected Communist
by the Patrol Officer Evans.
For the next weeks she sends tomato juice
his favourite – sardines
biscuits and Vegemite.

Word comes Bruno is dying.
He requests Olive come.

She writes urgently to the Governor.[14]
'It is most upsetting
to get messages from him to say
that he wants to see me and yet
I am prevented from going.
So please cut this heartless "red tape"
and yourself give me permission (by wire)
on the grounds of decent human feeling…'

After much bureaucratic hufflepuff
red tape is cut.
A telegram arrives:
'Miss Pink has permission for daily visits.'[15]

Olive rushes to Bruno's side
He is weak but knows her
gives her some papers. They chat.

His grandchildren hold Olive's hand.
Some walk back along the Todd with her.
She promises to return next day.

Greatest honour ever

Olive looks through Bruno's papers.
There is a signed note for her:
Bruno calls her '*Chidjadda'allardijar*',
scribbling an explanation,

'Like one tree – them come along shade,
everybody to that *Chidjadda*.
Bruno
December 22nd 1951 age 97.[16]

'He says this of me!' Olive whispers
in a shaky voice.
'This is one of the greatest honours ever.'

Overcome with grief
she folds it and writes across it,
'I must keep this – valuable
…a very high compliment
and great honour coming from
a full blood Arrernte man.'[17]
She vows to visit him everyday.

But it is the slow footsteps
of Bruno's family
early next dawn, that tell her it is too late.
His granddaughter holds Olive's hand tightly.
There are no words.

In her letter to Paul Hasluck she writes,
'It is an end. With Bruno dying, history has passed,
for he remembered, as a young boy
seeing the explorer Stuart
go through his own country in 1862 –
the first white man
any of his tribe had ever seen.'[18]

An uncertain future

Other army huts fill up.
A group of rowdy workmen
move in next door.
Nine years of seclusion and peace
abruptly end.

Loud music, swearing, midnight parties
and horn-blowing bring Olive Pink
to breaking point.
It quickly becomes a major feud.

Laughter and name-calling and a fire
lit in a hedge on her side
causes panic. Sarcasm and teasing
bring their disputes to court.

Olive is unfairly blamed
for causing trouble.
Within the next month she is sacked
from her court job and given
an eviction notice from Home Hut.[19]

Olive sits in what has been her home
for so long, misery pressed into her brow.
She rocks back and forth
her mouth dry, eyes closed.
Questions crowd her mind.
How can she give up her hut and garden
the place she has created?

Eviction

How to abide this barrenness
in the centre of her chest?
Exposed as a windswept sand dune
she wraps her arms around herself,
closes her eyes.

The first eviction notice
in her hand
destroys her – no home, no income
condemned to poverty and homelessness.

Inspiration

Alone inside the hut
Olive awaits the final eviction.
In the turbulence of the night
a thought keeps surfacing
a stubborn cork on a choppy sea.
An idea beams through the fog
takes shape, points in a new direction.
She sits up in bed, heart racing.
'Yes. That is it.'

The pale light of dawn
tumbles through the gap
of her boarded-up window
its shafts frissons of optimism.
She strides to the court
seeks a licence
to pitch her tent on the vacant plot
near Billy Goat Hill
(the place where she got lost
weeks before).
She knows the exact spot she wants –
lying between two rocky ridges.
It catches the ever changing colours
of the Macdonnell Range.

It is quickly approved –
maybe because it's out of town
maybe because it's over the river
maybe because it is out of sight.

A new door creaks open, turning
on the hinge of her aching heart
rich with hope and expectation.

For Olive, banishment from the world
by the sword is into a future garden
maybe arid and barren
but in her vision an Eden.
A back to front genesis story –
a mote of freedom beams in her eyes.

Thunder raining poison

'Two thousand, two thousand or more
tears we cried for our Land
for the fear you gave us,
for the sickness and the dying.'[20]

Olive hears Reg Harris pull up
in the old ute. He calls out to her
an agitated edge on his voice.
'We have lost, Miss Pink.
The land is declared…
a nuclear testing bomb site –
at Maralinga Tjarutja.'[21]
Olive's eyes darken, shakes her head
'But it's Pitjantjatjara country.
I know that land. I know its people.
They can't do it. It is not possible.'

They go inside. Olive fills the kettle.
'A cup of tea is what we need.'
Reg dunks his biscuit, they sit in silence.
She rubs her thumb and forefinger
across the bridge of her nose
shakes her head over and over –
her worst fear creeping in
like a cold draught on a winter's day.

She stirs her tea.
She has feared Americans
using the country, now the British.
Something prickly sinks into the pit
of her stomach. She hunches in discomfort.

Olive thinks of the land around Ooldea,
the carefree laughter of the children
the dusty feet of dancing men in red sand
flocks of chirping budgerigars at the spring.
Its foot print on her heart
now a blunt weapon crushing her chest.

Over the next weeks her protests are ignored.
Out of sight out of mind, city people could say.
Just as witnesses turn their back on the blasts
Australia turns its back on this piece of history.

'Two thousand, two thousand or more
trees dead with arms to the sky.
all the birds missing. no birdsong here
just stillness.'[22]

13
Creating a garden
1955–1973

A new fire kindles

If it is true that dark clouds
have silver linings
this one has a gold lining
for many of the townsfolk
including John Hargrave
call out the injustice
and rally to support Olive.

It takes all day, with a truck, an old ute
ferrying back and forth across the Todd.
But there is poetry in moving house
when it is communal.
Dr John Hargrave wishing to assist
packs Olive's personal things into his car
and is bogged twice in the dust of the Todd.
The drums of plants take sheer force.
With strain of muscle and faces taut
there is hullabaloo enough
to be heard all over town.
Many Warlpiri people help
add extra excitement to the day.

They erect Olive's tent
in the shade of old bean trees.
She sets her couch and table
and gazes with an artist's eye –
caught by the flourish of colour.

As the sun drops out of sight
they kindle a fire
and late into the night they all sit around
full of stories. The night swells with laughter.

For the next two years with the genesis
of her garden, Olive lives in a tent.
She visualises her empty Home Hut
re-erected on this spot and writes letters
imploring authorities to sell it to her.

A burgeoning solution evolves.
The Governor finds,
'…because Olive has paid rent
for over nine years, she can buy it,
dismantled, for five pounds.'
She has won. It is 1955. Olive
has her Home Hut on her land.[1]

A déjà vu moment

Olive finds her town planning skills
from fifty years back very useful.
She writes to her niece,
'I visualise a great garden
to preserve the fragile flora
that is so quickly disappearing.
I look forward to your visit.'
Olive bemoans how she is getting old –
'Life is sitting on my chest at present
too much to do with too little time
and too little energy – with this daily heat.'[2]

At dusk watching the sky scatter its stars
she hears a rustle of leaves
the beam-light eyes of the Warlpiri man
who rescued her that first day
shine from the tangled scrub.

'Missus, my job at the bungalow is no good.
I have a family and need a proper wage…
My name is Jampijimpa…Johnny
I will be your gardener.'[3]
Olive jumps from her reverie.
He bows to her, his cap in hand.
Something like a flutter of butterflies stirs
in her belly. Her vision could be a reality!

'Jampijimpa, when could you start?'
He answers without hesitation,
'At dawn, missus.'

'At dawn it is,' she says shaking his hand.
'You will be paid a proper wage.'
He gives her a harvest moon smile.
A month or so later, she writes to her niece,
'I have a straight and fine man behind me now.
He is a Warlpiri man and a family man –
we are working together.'[4]

Creating the garden

Routine settles in, breathes with purpose.
Rising at 4 a.m.
over a cup of tea and honeyed cakes
cooked on the hot coals from last night's fire
Jampijinpa and Olive plan their day.
He digs her irrigation project
wide eyed with amazement
while Olive waters, weeds
tends the delicate seedlings
in a makeshift nursery.

'Patience with small details,'
says Olive, 'will make perfect a large work.'

They face a litany of daily hurdles –
goats, rabbits, stray cattle, all nibble
at lush shoots and greenery.
Children climb in and take fruit.
Drought stalks, ever ready to pounce.

Chicken wire and an illegal cactus hedge
cannot deter all enemies
but her water conservation networks
fortify her 'home garden' –
greens, herbs and flowers.

She hones her versatility
to design and landscape her reserve –
layout of avenues, stands of trees
with draw-off and collecting ponds.
Olive's plans are aesthetically pleasing.

She writes to a friend,
'I am already growing Sturt desert pea,
cassia and native hibiscus
and I want a stand of ghost gums!'[5]

My own Papinya

Refreshed as morning dew
a new dream percolates – she visualises
this crown land gazetted as a Flora Reserve.
She writes to Minister Hasluck
and sends him an invitation to visit.
His letter of thanks arrives.

Instinctively Olive jots down
a strategy to entertain
and charm the minister!

She plans the optimum time of day
when the sky is a palette of colour
after the flies
before the odd mosquito.
Olive wants him to appreciate the peace
and experience the glory
of the sun setting over Mt Gillen.

She finds her lace cloth,
sets out her best white china.
In the fire oven she cooks a madeira cake
and local fig and date loaf.

Not only is the minister charmed
fourteen acres of land are gazetted
and he asks Olive to be 'the honorary curator'
of the first Arid Flora Reserve in the world.[6]

'I had longed to return one day
to Papinya in the desert
where I had been so happy,'
she writes again to her nieces,
'but my age has prevented that.
Now I have my own Papinya
here in Alice Springs.'[7]

Water-wise garden

Olive beams when she walks country
collecting seeds. In her 'nursery'
she waits for them to germinate
as a parent would tend new babies.

She identifies, sketches,
checks Indigenous use of each plant –
for food, medicine and ritual.

Everyday the shifting raptor of water
clutches them in its talons
like a wedged-tail eagle
chokes its prey on wing.
Olive and Jampijinpa struggle to be free –
using eight-gallon drums and more ponds
to collect rare water
gutters to channel it.
They sink pipes into the ground
at the base of each tree
and Olive watches the garden
create its own terrarium effect
to protect itself against drought.[8]

She writes,
'I worship trees and flowers.
And especially the 'gallant' ones
of the arid regions of Australia.
I love doing the work on it
and it is the most beautiful spot
in Alice Springs.

It is for future generations –
a place of peace and beauty for the people.
And I encourage and plant
as many arid plants as I can get
(and at 75 have strength for!).
We have planted numerous mulga
and forty more Sturt bean trees.
When the bean trees become big enough
to give shade, sand can be placed
for children to play under the trees.
It will be a reserve for people
to wander about, for the nurses
from the hospital to sit and rest.'[9]

Olive gives trees names of politicians –
when she is angry, they don't get watered
and she informs them by letter![10]

When the Minister Hasluck votes
in favour of the Assimilation Policy in parliament[11]
which Olive vocally opposes as pernicious
he receives a strident letter –
'He is no longer being watered and will
probably die in this heat!'[12]

An acquired bath

Late in 1962 rushed renovations
begin on the Administrator's house.

Queen Elizabeth and Prince Phillip
are to make a two-day visit inland!
Six new baths are to be installed
for the visiting Royal party!

Olive writes to the paper
of the 'wicked waste of money
especially in Alice Springs!'

Then a shift in her next letter to her niece,
'I have scored one of the old baths formerly for VIPs.
I have been given one! so I am delighted.
Better than an OBE.'[13]

Olive turns eighty

As dryness intensifies into drought
and 'a killer heat' drains
Olive rises at 4 a.m.
and works till sunrise.

Eleven years of reading the seasons
of listening to the earth
of experiencing its rhythms
familiar with its cycles
struggling for sustainability
takes its toll.
Now three gardeners in rotation
water, mulch and work the garden.

Word spreads –
Olive now 80 years old is not well.
Her heart ailment means
she is seen less at the courthouse
where she gets respite in the cool.

When Reg Harris the local electrician
hears Olive is not well he speaks up for her.
'She's a good soul. She creates a beautiful garden.
Already tourists come and ask to see it.
We should help her.
Make her more comfortable.'

He rallies a group of local men
sends her off for the day reassuring her,
'The materials are second-hand.
I don't want you bossing me around.'

It is Australia Day 1964.
They line the walls with used sheeting
paint it pale blue
install a phone
a fluorescent light, an electric cooler for her food
and the *pièce de résistance,*
a second-hand air conditioner.

With a chuckle she calls her Home Hut 'the ice box'
and writes to her nieces,
'It is almost a miracle. I feel a renewed person
I have so many friends and helpers.'

An enduring gardener

Olive has always been a gardener.
She has created
and tendered gardens
leaving them as gifts for newcomers
and for the healing of the planet.[14]

Her letters describe her new garden.
Bulbs are sprouting, hyacinths and gladdies
the shape of tongues and green melons.
Tomatoes and lots of herbs
flourish in drums under bean tree shade.
'This spring,' she adds,
'most of the herbs
and flowers I will sell to hotels
but what I am most proud of are eighteen sapling gums
and the young mulga I grew from seed.
With my understanding (although I am no botanist)
and with the knowledge of the black gardeners
that work with me,
we are succeeding.'[15]

She has always a next step
a new vision
and loyal, hard-working gardeners.
Tonight the brawny spring moon
gives her light for working in coolness.
She knows the bird and frog call for rain –
their welcoming song a joy to her ears.
She prepares seedlings to receive it.

She takes old milk tins, cuts out the bottom,
punches holes in the lids
adds the composted soil
and seedlings.
As they grow
she will take off lids
planting them sheathed into the ground
without disturbing the roots!
An OMP invention!

For Olive a new calm settles.
The past stresses slough away
as bark peels from trees and snakes shed skin.

14
A first arid garden
1974

A social justice warrior

Sheila, a regular friend from town,
pops in for a cup of tea.
Olive is settled at her old army table
amidst boxes of correspondence
opened bottles of ink – red, green and black.
She is proud of a finished letter
to the Darwin Administrator.
The page is full – it shouts
with coloured inks, underlines,
up the margin, down the other side.

Sheila knows Olive receives hundreds
of Christmas cards and hampers
from all over Australia, but is impressed
to see Canberra correspondence.

With eyes deep as wells, Olive enthuses,
'I have this hunger for justice.
Full-blood Aborigines in our country
deserve hope. My ideas are contentious
now but I believe the government
will soon listen.'

Yet the core of Olive's arguments
lies outside conventional frameworks,
her voice echoes an arid wilderness.[1]
She knows she moves to a different tune
yet she steels herself.

Hope carries her spirit.
Maybe it lands exhausted in the dust
but like the prodigal
it returns from squandered efforts
with small patches of possibility.

When she storms to the courthouse
demanding explanations
she watches men slink behind their desks.
She laughingly tells Sheila of one,
'who crawled along the floor
claiming not to be in!'

Olive ambles with Sheila around the garden
points out eco-friendly plans and tells her stories.

Sheila knows there is a division of opinion
among the local townsfolk
Miss Pink – idealist or eccentric![2]

Sheila admires her tenacity.
Around town she stands up for Olive.
She knows as the sun rises in the east
Olive's sincerity is unwavering.

Jampijinpa Yannarilyi (Johnny)

Olive's vision ignites
Jampijinpa's passion for gardening.

Being her very first gardener
he is proud of their creation –
a beautiful place
with designed pathways, plantings
and seats from the natural stone, placed
to watch the sun set behind the range.

He works hard, resists the alcohol curse
that is toxic to many in town.
He is proud when Olive helps him
reclaim his name
–Yannarilyi –
the name of a hill and soakage
of his maternal grandfather's totemic country.

When the scourge of alcohol
finally grips him
Olive finds him respite – to dry out.
Back at the garden he remains unwell
fit only for light chores.

They apply for a form of army pension.
He is refused.
'"271 Johnny" had the honorary rank
of corporal,
served in uniform nearly four years
from 1942
but was never formally a soldier'![3]

Olive is outraged. Once more
her sense of justice is offended.
All her avenues of protest are brick-walled.
Letters to authorities go unanswered.

A few months later
her story with this gentle man ends.
His family stand bereft before her.
Olive mourns with them.
'Our garden is his legacy'
is her only consolation.

Olive works through her grief –
as she plans a brass plate in his honour,

'Johnny Jampijinpa Yannarilyi
a Warlpiri man made this reserve.
A native-born botanist and etymologist
whose knowledge of local plants
and growing conditions was invaluable to me,
                    September 1974'[4]

Being stubborn

Olive's friends write of skirmishes
and shootings of Aborigines
that hardly get a mention in the papers.

She is alert at her court visits.
Injustice constantly asserts itself.
No apology.
No undersatanding.
No compromise.
Like an ogre it shouts
blocks any bridge Olive attempts
to cross. It sits with her every evening.
She confronts it in her letters to the paper
calls it out for what it is.

Injustice is stubborn
as she is accused of being stubborn
when she insists her gardeners
be paid regular and just wages.

'Miss Pink, you are a very difficult person'
comes the reply from Darwin.
'You are a troublemaker'
comes another, when she uses her voice
for the voiceless. 'She is dangerous,'
says another, fearing
she has 'communist' tendencies.[5]

Olive always finds a new fight
yet her eyes darken.
There is much to do
and her stamina is running out.

The first garden party

A Sunday in autumn.
Respite from summer heat.
Olive celebrates by dressing in white.
She reminisces how she missed it
in the desert where everything
had a pinkish tinge.
She looks in the tiny wall mirror.
The smile is lost, the eyes look tired.
She stares at herself
defeated by the onslaught of age.

She rolls her hair back
tucks it up smoothly
ties the collar bow with resolve.

Olive is 90 years old.
Today she is pleased to be alive
but wonders for how much longer!
She wants no fuss.
Sheila said she will stop by.
Even when some of the Warlpiri women
set up their camp at the back of the garden
she is unsuspecting.

The air is electric
yet she still suspects nothing.
Sheila arrives for a cup of tea.
By mid-afternoon
on the mildest most beautiful day of the year
twenty people cross the Todd
bringing a party atmosphere with them.

The billy boils, tea is made
a Madeira cake adorns the table.
Reg Harris and the men arrive
with a flagon of sherry and one of port wine.
The first garden party of the Reserve begins.

Sitting in her garden, her labour of love
for twenty years, Olive allows a last photo
to be taken.

15
The circle of life
1975

We shall not cease from exploration
And the end of all our exploring
Will be to arrive where we started
And know the place for the first time
– T.S. Eliot

The paradox of OMP

Olive is a charming lady –
to some.
She loves to serve a cup of tea
talk of books, music, art and plants.
Olive is a loyal friend –
to many.
Everyone knows
of the newsy letters and cards
from her nieces and many friends
that settle snugly on her shelves.

Yet the private, passionate OMP
presents a threatening figure.
In a world of us and them
she trespasses
from the frontier norm
weaves her improbable way.

Her stature is an anachronism
her writings reflect Victorian ways
and leave her open to criticism.
Olive is scorned
but unrelenting in her call
for equality and justice.

She smiles when she thinks
how she has kept the magistrates on their toes
and how they make sure they have interpreters,
'In case Miss Pink should arrive'.

Joy of family

Tiredness tugs, stirs into 1975.
Olive becomes more and more reclusive.
She writes to her nieces of her winter days
in this summer heat.

Her eldest niece 'hot and hatless'
arrives with a driver at the garden's entrance
walks the red sandy path
to a barrier of chicken wire
with a sign,
'No admittance by order'.
She smiles, makes her way through
calls out to her aunt.

Another gate tied with rope and another sign,
'The Honorary Curator is unwell
and is not to be disturbed on Saturday or Sunday.
Her telephone number is…if you must.'
She knocks and calls again.
She later writes,
'The windows were all boarded-up.
I could only imagine the darkness inside.'[1]

Again she knocks.
'Come in. If you don't mind seeing
a wreck. I'll open the door.'
And she did and she was.

'Her warm smile and sense of humour
could not hide her frailty.
Her hair was lank and grey
gathered strands piled on her head,
while a nightdress and old grey coat
betrayed wrinkled stockings.
She kissed me warmly and said,
"Don't live till you're this old."
And we had tea.'[2]

Olive has her affairs in order.[3]
She gives her niece all her papers
with writings, sketches, paintings
boxed for the Tasmanian University.[4]

Arm in arm they walk slowly
around the garden.
Olive points out trees and plants
introduces the gardeners.
They sit in the shade.
'Oh, you are a darling to come and visit me.
I am so proud of you, proud of my three nieces.'

They join the driver
knowing they would not meet again.
Her niece later wrote,
'My aunt remained with a gardener
waving until I was out of view.'[5]

Dangerous Miss Pink

Her appearances are rare now.
The gardeners often work near her hut
and listen for movement.

Today when Olive steps out
one of the men leaves the gully
where he is digging a new channel
and comes to her side –
she takes his arm for a short stroll.
Breathless, her steps mindful, slow.
She sits while he replaces
a few stray stones at the Corkwood tree
she labelled 'Mr Hasluck'.

She reminisces aloud,
'Sheila says they call me eccentric.
It's probably true.'
They both laugh.
'I used every means with pen and ink
to bring injustice to public attention
and keep it to the fore.'
Her lips curl. A hesitant smile.
'They called me dangerous!'
He levels out some of the stones.
They sit a while in the stillness.

She turns, puts her hand on his arm,
'The garden is glorious.
I am leaving. But you must stay,
and insist you keep getting proper pay.'

They walk further
sit on a chiselled stone seat
and watch the colours on the hills
as the sun begins its journey home.

The veil

At dusk Olive makes a cup of tea
laced with medicinal brandy
and sits quietly.
She listens to the shemozzle
of roosting birds
the chatter of the gardeners' families
as they prepare evening meals
and a distant ring of laughter
from the groups around low ember fires
down on the dry Todd.
The last wallabies
come in closer, tame in her presence.

In the coolness
she makes one last walk
slowly to the gate
and looks towards the Todd.
How she loves this river
with its cool channels of air
in the stinging heat.
She remembers the few times she saw it flood
with its bird-coloured sky
and raucous sounds of delight.

Tonight the luminous sky
reminds her of Celtic stories
where the air is thinly veiled
between heaven and earth.

Her dim desert eyes
search an emu-watching sky.
The Seven Sisters beckon[6]
in coolamon dark.
She watches the Milky Way
slowly flow into a path –
an invitation.

Olive's limbs are tired
her heart worn out.
Love for the earth and for these people
are only long inner conversations.

Autumn 1975

There is a clockwork grief
a slowness of forever
day and night morphing
into the sense that life is as brief
as the whiff of a candle.

The hills assume their nightfall personality.
Inky silhouettes against the blue-black sky
confer a comforting gravitas.

Olive ponders,
'Of all the ample gifts of my garden
perhaps now the most precious is silence,'[7]
and wonders who she would be
without the nourishment of this quiet.
'So precious is this gift
it feels to me like an element in and of itself.
I wonder if it is the intimacy with the garden
that connects with some still eternal part of me
and makes me believe that I will be heard.'[8]

It has been a struggle
keeping this park as an arid reserve
as the council tries to interfere.

'If they had their way,' she once told a visitor,
'we would have rows of oleanders
and coloured seats
and the natural stillness of this country
would be smothered.
We have to keep it as it is – an arid garden.'[9]

She hears an owl calling
too weary to go out to search
just thrilled that the big-eyed, heart-shaped face
of the barn owl is in her garden.

Tomorrow she will write another letter
to emphasise the vulnerability and unique beauty –
the importance of preserving arid flora.

Bringing the light

And when you have reached the mountain top,
then you shall begin to climb.
And when the earth shall claim your limbs,
then shall you truly dance.
– Kahlil Gibran, *The Prophet*

Olive can no longer fork the earth in her garden –
no longer carry water to her hungry progeny.
Now she can only dedicate her garden for peace
for children to play in
for people to wander
for the stressed to sit
bathed in the aura of nature.
Again she closes herself off
with gates and chicken wire.
Too weak to cook she lives on cups of tea
milk arrowroot biscuits
and her medicinal brandy.

After a few days she struggles from her bed
calls a gardener
to knock out the boarded planks of the window.
A delicate glow from Mt Gillen radiates across her face.
Her mountain.
She remembers her bookplate –
the ideal of it!
Olive climbs with her torch aflame.

Going home

She imagines the whole tin wall opening
to her garden and mountain.
The rising of the sun
brings hope –
flashes of iridescent butterflies
chirping from the water tank
laughter of children.
Wedge-tails dare the updrafts
hover on the thermals, in and out of view.
Flies assault tenaciously
as she fixes her fly net.

Olive hears a measured beat on the ground –
sees Mick and Bruno dancing.
A chimera of young smiling men
their eyes alive with spirit.
Pervasive dust blankets the air
sets to rise again.

It films on her teeth, she tastes it
senses the warmth of the campfire
as the billy boils and hot cakes smoulder
in the coals and the effusive
smiling Warlpiri women
lace them with their harvested honey.
Time has lost its depth. Time has lost
its perspective all overlapping
tumbling versions of the now –
the only passage of time.

So much learnt over cups of tea
and madeira cake. Her courage
holds close like precious drops of water.
She shuts her eyes. Drifts off untroubled
everything clear, and radiant.
Undaunted, daring, determined
she dreams her quest for justice.

The light shifts
colour-glint from the mountain.
In the sun's haze a snowcapped
childhood mountain emerges in a fog.
She feels Kunanyi's cold.

Among wildflowers a young girl walks
with her father. He beckons her
pauses to show her a local plant.
A Warlpiri woman, her face familiar
fades in, smiles and points,
'The corkwood tree, your totem.'

They stroll in the garden
with comfort and ease.
'Yes, the miracle from seed.'

At first she sees them then only hears them.
'From under their feet the dust flies
their leg muscles quiver
the hills sway
to the rhythm of the moon
to seasons
in turns of light and dark
all as one
one as all with the earth.'

Olive is home.

Epilogue

After a few days of silence, Sheila comes knocking. Olive lies peacefully, half conscious, her net covering her face. By the time she alerts Olive's friends and they transport her to hospital, Olive has passed. It is 6 July 1975.

As she wished, a local Quaker, John Newland, conducted her funeral and she was buried as she had instructed, her grave facing towards her beloved Mount Gillen, in the opposite direction to all the other graves.[1] She had reserved the plot in the non-denominational section of the Alice Springs Cemetery and told her nieces that there would be 'no flowers'. A small flower is, however, carved into her simple gravestone and she did instruct her friend and benefactor, Reg Harris, that his wife 'may place a bunch of violets' on her casket.[2]

Some twenty-one friends attended her funeral. Most of them went to Harris's home afterwards, to be served sherry, a cup of tea and Madeira cake, just as Olive served it to her visitors at Home Hut.

In death, as in her life, she demonstrated her individuality, independence, strength and great love of nature.

'Her grave looks out onto the magnificent red and blue cragginess of the McDonnell Range, out towards the desert and the Aboriginal land that she loved. Her work on behalf of Aboriginal Australians, her anthropological research into Arrernte land ownership and her labour of love of her flora reserve, live on.'[3]

> Vale Miss Pink, friend of 45 years.
> You can now paint the flowers
> in God's Garden of Eden.
>
> – Horrie Simpson

Chronology

1884	Olive is born in Hobart on 17 March.
1888	Olive's brother Eldon is born.
1890–3	Olive attends Miss Ayton's School for Girls (art and sculpture classes).
1894	Olive attends Hobart Girls' School and Hobart Technical School.
1907	Olive's father dies.
1911	Olive and her mother follow Eldon to Perth to take up farming. Olive sets up her own art studio.
1913	Olive is betrothed to a Tasmanian friend, Harold Southern.
1914	World War I begins. Harold enlists and sails for Egypt. Olive moves with her mother to Sydney. Olive offers art lessons privately.
1915	Olive is employed by the Department of Public Works as a tracer. Harold is killed at Gallipoli. She joins the Red Cross. She attends Julian Ashton Art School in Sydney. She studies for a Town Planning Diploma, and is employed by Government Railways & Tramways, designing advertising posters.
1926	Olive makes her first journey inland. She becomes interested in how Indigenous people are treated. She has a five-week stay in Ooldea with Daisy Bates.
1927–8	Olive is a foundation member of the Anthropological Society of NSW.
1929	Olive's mother dies.
1930	Olive makes her second inland journey, six months. She becomes interested in the well-being of the Arrernte and Warlpiri peoples.

1931	Olive studies for a Diploma in Anthropology at Sydney University.
1932	Olive gives a paper at the ANZAAS Congress in Sydney.
1933	Olive makes her third journey inland, one month, to complete her research thesis.
1934	Olive has her Diploma in Anthropology and her first research grant. She makes her fourth journey inland, twelve months, on her research grant.
1935	Olive gives two papers at the ANZAAS Congress in Melbourne.
1936	Olive spends close to a year in Hobart to write up her research.
1940	Olive makes her fifth and final journey inland. She makes the inland her home. She becomes welfare worker for the Arrernte and Warlpiri peoples.
1942–46	Olive moves to Thompson's Rockhole and lives in community with the Warlpiri. She awaits the outcome of an application for a lease of land for a 'secular sanctuary'.
1947	Olive moves back into Alice Springs and rents an ex-army hut on Gregory Terrace. She becomes a cleaner at the courthouse and calls out injustices of the day. As an activist, she continues writing letters to authorities and media.
1955	Olive is evicted from Gregory Terrace and applies for a piece of land near Billy Goat Hill on the east side of the Todd River. She is granted a licence to occupy a half acre of Crown Land 'for gardening purposes'. She campaigns for surrounding land to be set aside in perpetuity as a reserve.

1956	The land is gazetted as the Australian Arid Regions Flora Reserve. Olive is its first curator.
1956–75	Olive and her Warlpiri assistant gardeners develop the gardens, working in drought conditions and within funding constraints. She demands equal rights for Aborigines, and equal pay and conditions for her gardeners and other Aboriginal workers.
1975	Olive dies. The NT government assumes control and sets about fulfilling her vision of a public area for the appreciation of native flora.
1985	The gardens are reopened to the public as the Olive Pink Flora Reserve.
1988	Olive is honoured as a Pioneer of the Northern Territory. Her name is included in 200 tiles for the Bicentennial Walkway in the Darwin Park.
1995	The gardens are listed on the National Estate.
1996	The gardens are renamed Olive Pink Botanic Garden.
2009	The gardens are included in the Northern Territory Heritage Register.
2012	After much lobbying from her family, Olive's tile on the Pioneer walk is changed from 'eccentric' to 'Anthropologist'.

Glossary

Afghan Express (the Ghan) reached remote Oodnadatta in 1891, where an itinerant population of around 150 Afghan cameleers were based.

Albrecht, Friedrich Wilhelm Pastor (1894–1984) was a Lutheran missionary and pastor at Hermannsburg Mission in Central Australia from 1926 to 1952. He met Olive and she found they had the physical needs of the Arrernte people in common. His understanding of their spirituality differed from Olive and made her angry.

Alice Springs (Mparntwe) is situated roughly in Australia's geographical centre.

Ampetyane, Ned was an Arrernte man from the far west. He spoke Arrernte and Warlpiri and English so he carried respect to assist Olive in entering the country.

ANRC: Australian National Research Council.

ANZAAS: Australian and New Zealand Association for the Advancement of Science (founded in 1886). Olive made it a forum for discussion about Aboriginal concerns and gave papers uniting her two passions, Indigenous welfare and arid flora.

Arrernte people are a group of Aboriginal Australians who live in the Arrernte lands, near Mparntwe in the Central Australia region of the Northern Territory.

Assimilation Policy (1951–1962) was a policy of absorbing Aboriginal people into white society through the process of removing children from their families.

Association for the Protection of Native Races (APNR) was formed in 1911 by William Morley, a Congregational minister, to raise awareness and improve the conditions of Aborigines in Australia. Olive joined it in its formative years.

Bandicoot Man was the totem of Mick Dow Dow.

Barrenjoey Lighthouse is a prominent light in Sydney, built 1881. It comes from the word for a young kangaroo in the language of the local Gadagil people.

Bates, Daisy (1863–1951) was a journalist and welfare worker among Aborigines. She dedicated her life to the welfare of the Indigenous people that she lived with, writing over 200 articles about them, and was an early inspiration for Olive. Olive and Daisy met at the 1926 ANZAAS Conference.

Bengers Liquid Food was a pre-digestive food.

Billy Goat Hill was the early colonial name for Annie Meyers Hill in Olive Pink Botanical Garden. (Olive encouraged the renaming.) It is now designated Tharrarletneme (Warlpiri) Akeyyulerre (Arrernte). The **Bohemian Circle** was a group which practised an unconventional lifestyle involving musical, artistic, literary and spiritual pursuits.

Braitling, R.R. (William) (?–1959) was a pastoralist who took up traditional Warlpiri land incorporating Pikilyu, an important sacred site. He was an antagonist for Olive.

Caledon Bay, NT was the site of a crisis which was the impetus for a lot of agitation and letter writing, and new awareness of injustice and inequality.

Cameleers were Afghan camel drivers, also known as 'Afghans' or 'Ghans', who worked in outback Australia from 1860 to the 1930s.

Campbell, Stormy was maybe a half-caste Aborigine, living in Alice Springs, who enjoyed the adventure with Olive on expeditions and being on her payroll.

Caterpillar Dreaming comes from an Arrernte Aboriginal people's Dreamtime story. It involves the creation of the East and West Macdonnell Ranges that shelter the town of Alice Springs.

Chilla Well (also Jila) is a Warlpiri soakage on the Tanami Track north-west of Alice Springs.

Claypan squatters were men who mined the tailings after the mine was finished.

Cleland, J.B. Professor (1878–1971) had a chair at University of Adelaide. He met Olive through a letter of introduction from her Tasmanian friend Dr William Crowther, a family friend, confidant and supporter.

Coniston Massacre took place near the Coniston cattle station in the Territory of Central Australia from 14 August to 18 October 1928. It was the last known officially sanctioned massacre of Indigenous Australians during the Australian Frontier Wars.

Coniston Station was a picturesque and productive station of 2,170 square kilometres, 285 kilometres north-west of Alice Springs with reliable water. During the drought of 1928–29, the Aboriginal peoples gravitated back towards the ancient river source which the pastoralists needed for their cattle. Conflict arose.

Cooee! is a shout used in Australia, usually in the bush, to attract attention, find missing people, or indicate one's own location. It was used on call-out posters for World War I.

corkwood is a gnarled tree which can grow six metres high with thick, fissured bark. The cream to pale yellow flower spikes often appear in winter. The thick bark insulates the trunk and protects it from fire, enabling it to survive and regrow new shoots afterwards. Mick gives Olive the corkwood tree as her totem.

Crowther, William Dr (1887–1981) was director of the Tasmanian Museum and Art Gallery for fifty-five years, and a confidant and supporter of Olive. He introduced Olive by letter to Professor J.B. Cleland in Adelaide.

Darwin is the capital city of the Northern Territory. In the 1930s it was the centre of governance for the northern end of Australia.

Dechineux, Lucien (1869-1957) was a painter, architect and sculptor, born in Belgium. He arrived in Australia at the age of fifteen in 1884. In 1907, he became Principal of Hobart Technical School and was part of Olive's inspiration in art.

Doctor Biffin's Special Heart Tonic: Dr Elisa Biffin (1868–1939) was one of the first woman doctors in Sydney. 'The war left many Sydney women bereaved and one of these was Greenwich resident and anthropologist Olive Pink, who sought Biffin's services after her sweetheart was killed at Gallipoli. In 1916, Biffin prescribed a special tonic for Olive's heart condition, a prescription Pink took for the rest of her life.' (*The Dictionary of Sydney*)

Doreen Station, Mount, is a cattle station north-west of Alice Springs just off the Tanami Track in the central region of the Northern Territory (see Braitling above). Olive lobbied against their acquiring the lease. The Warlpiri people received recognition for their native title of the area in 2014. The initial application had been filed with the Federal Court in 2005.

Dow Dow, Bruno (?–1951) was a Warlpiri man who had early experience with European settlers, and a grasp of English. He and his brother Mick formed the foundation of Olive's anthropological research team.

Dow Dow, Jim and Charlie were brothers of Mick and Bruce Dow Dow, Warlpiri guides.

Dow Dow, Mick was a Warlpiri guide. Olive called him an 'Indigenous anthropologist'.

Dreaming describes for Australian Indigenous people 'how the Ancestral Beings moved across the land naming significant geographic features. Dreaming stories pass on important knowledge, cultural values and belief systems. Through song, dance, painting and storytelling which express the dreaming stories, Aborigines have maintained a link with the Dreaming from ancient times to today, creating a rich cultural heritage which could be called philosophy today.' (Dr Victoria Grieve-Williams, a Warrainaay woman from mid north coast NSW on ABC *Blueprint for Living* 2019)

Edwards Crossing Siding was an old Ghan railway siding near Bungadilla Creek. Edward Creek Station was built in 1889 as one of the more significant maintenance centres along the Great Northern Railway.

Elkin, A.P., Professor (1891–1979) was an Anglican pastor and influential Australian anthropologist. He became Professor of Anthropology at Sydney University.

Female Factory (1828–1856) was a former Australian workhouse for female convicts in Hobart.

fettler (from the word settler) was one who worked on the railway track in the outback.

fly-net hat is a bush hat with netting. Olive wore one most of her life.

Ghan is a long-distance train from Adelaide to Darwin, named in memory of the camel drivers working in the outback in the nineteenth century.

Granites is a gold mining region on the edge of the Tanami Desert, Northern Territory.

Haast's Bluff, 230 kilometres west of Alice Spring, is nestled within the West MacDonnell Ranges in Central Australia.

Hargrave, John, a good friend and confidant of Olive, went to Alice Springs in 1956 as a researcher into Aboriginal health.

Harris, Reg was a local Alice Springs resident (possibly an electrician). He was a loyal friend to Olive.

Hasluck, Paul Sir 1905–1993) was Minister for Territories.

He respected Olive Pink, giving her time, reading her letters, visiting. He approved the fourteen acres gazetted for the reserve, making Olive honorary curator of the park.

Hermannsburg Mission (1877–1982) was where Lutheran missionaries established a school and dormitories for children in the late 1890s. The land was returned to the local Arrente people in 1982.

Hobart/nipalua (gazetted dual name) is capital of Tasmania. Its duel name is an act of reconciliation. The name comes from the revived Aboriginal language of palawa kani.

Hovea montana is a short-stemmed branching shrub. Pea-like deep mauve flowers occur profusely in spring in Tasmania.

Jampijinpa Yannarilyi (Johnny) (?–1973) was Olive's first gardener.

Japaljarri was a Warlpiri elder who lived on camp.

Junction Waterhole is on Crown Land and has wonderful views of Mt Gillen.

Kangaroo Ancestral Dance is part of the Dreaming.

Kramer, Ernest was a Swiss missionary, friends with the Strehlows. Olive made his acquaintance at the ANZAAS conference. She felt he betrayed her plans to the Strehlow.

Kunanyi is the dual name for Mt Wellington, the mountain overlooking Hobart

Lasseter's search was an unsuccessful search for explorer/prospector Harold Bell Lasseter in 1929 and 1930, lost while searching for a promised rich gold deposit in a desolate corner of Central Australia.

Line Party Bob was an Arrernte guide for Olive on her expedition north.

mallee is a low-growing bushy Australian eucalypt with slender stems.

Maralinga, in the west of South Australia, was the 3,300-square-kilometre site of British nuclear tests in the mid-1950s.

Meyers, Annie (1880–?) ran a well-known guest house in Alice Springs.

Mount Gillen is a striking landform in the Macdonnell Ranges.

Mparntwe is the Indigenous name for Alice Springs.

mulga tree grows to a height of ten metres but, in arid regions with low rainfall, it tends to reach three metres.

Munyani was an elder of the Warlpiri.

munyeroo is a succulent and valuable drought-resistant plant whose seeds and leaves are used for food.

Muyu is a Warlpiri medicine man with special knowledge of the plants and animals for healing medicine.

Namatjira, Albert (1902–1959) was a Western Arrernte-speaking Aboriginal artist from the Macdonnell Ranges in Central Australia.

Nullargi was a Warlpiri hunter who worked with Olive on her first year of research at Yunmaji Waterhole.

Nunguri was a young Pitjantjatjara man who met Olive at Oodnadatta station and took her onto his country when Elkin had let her down.

Oodnadatta is a remote outback town in South Australia, 873 kilometres north of Adelaide. For thousands of years it was a stop on an old trade route-songline for Aboriginal people.

Ooldea is a tiny settlement in South Australia. It is on the eastern edge of the Nullarbor Plain, 863 kilometres west of Port Augusta on the Trans-Australian Railway.

Orribinjer, Bob was a Warlpiri man who worked as guide and interpreter.

Owen, Sheila was a local resident of Alice Springs, a loyal friend of Olive.

Papyina is an area of Crown land with a large waterhole which Olive hoped could be secured as a safe haven for the Warlpiri, part of her plan for a 'secular sanctuary'.

Peltharre, Jack was a Warlpiri elder who went as interpreter on country with Olive.

Pikilyu is a waterhole near Haast's Bluff essential to Aboriginal survival. An important site for ceremonies, it is at the junction of a number of different Dreamings (jukurrpa), including Possum, Snake, Two Kangaroos, Flying Ant and Yam, which are today represented in the work of artist Kumantje Jagamara.

Pilbara strike: see footnote 11.3.

pitchi is an Indigenous word from the Western Desert, meaning a container made of wood or bark used for holding liquids or goods and sometimes a baby.

Pitjantjatara is an Aboriginal group of the Central Australian desert.

Port Arthur was a nineteenth-century penal settlement for convicts east of Hobart, 1833–1857.

Quakers (Friends) influenced Olive's formative years, hence her early inspiration to social justice and Aboriginal welfare and ideals of peace.

quandong is a native plant with edible fruit, also commonly referred to as a native peach.

Radcliffe-Brown, Alfred (1881–1955) was an English anthropologist. He was Professor of the new chair of Anthropology at the University of Sydney, 1926–1931.

Risdon Cove, a small bay front, was the site of an 1804 massacre, under the brooding eye of Kunanyi.

secular sanctuary was a term coined by Olive as a place where 'one can call their souls and bodies their own'.

Simpson, Horrie was a railway man with an interest in painting flowers. Olive and Horrie corresponded and stayed friends all her life.

soak is a source of water in Australian deserts.

Southern, Harold (1884?-1915) and his sister Muriel met Olive at Hobart Art School. She met him again in Perth before World War I. She was betrothed to him. He was killed at Gallipoli in 1915.

Southern, Muriel was Harold's sister whom Olive befriended in Sydney while they waited to hear from Harold.

specimen pouches are used to preserve plants destined for museums.

Stafford, Randal ran the station at Coniston and was acquainted with the white man 'Brooks, who was killed by the "blacks"'. This instigated the Coniston war, sanctioned by the government.

Stanner, W.E.H. (Bill) (1905–1981) was an Australian anthropologist who worked extensively with Indigenous Australians. He wrote *After the Dreaming* and is noted for giving the Boyer Lectures in 1968. He coined the words 'the Great Australian Silence'. The lectures were a pivotal moment in our history. 'Stanner's understanding came from an empathy and direct interaction with Aboriginal culture, and it was on 'his advice that former Prime Minister Gough Whitlam poured sand from his hand into that of Vincent Lingiari when handing the Wavehill Station back to the Gurindji people.' (Robert Manne)

Strehlow, T.G.H. (Ted) (1908–1978) was the son of a Lutheran missionary. He took expeditions into Arrernte country. Olive always felt their ways of viewing the Indigenous people differed.

Talkinjiya was the endearing name given to Olive by the Warlpiri people.

Tanami is Kukatja and Warlpiri country, north-west of Alice Springs. It is quite inhospitable to Europeans.

Tea and Sugar Rattler was an early name for the supply Ghan train from Adelaide

Thompson's Rockhole (Pirdi Piridi) is in the Tanami Desert, Northern Territory. Olive camped here 1942–1946 with the Warlpiri people.

totems are natural objects, plants or animals that are believed by a particular society to have spiritual significance.

tjurunga is an object of cultural significance to Central Australian Indigenous people of the Arrernte groups.

Tucker, Paddy and Topsy were Aborigines who had been on the Lasseter expedition and were happy to be on Olive's payroll.

Warlpiri people occupy an area north-west of Alice Springs and the area of the Tanami Desert. Today they live mainly in various towns and on Indigenously owned cattle stations.

Warlpiri language is spoken by about 3,000 of the Warlpiri people in the Northern Territory and is one of the largest Aboriginal languages in Australia in terms of number of speakers.

Wave Hill walk-off was a walk-off and strike by 200 Gurindji stockmen, house servants and their families starting in 1966 and lasting for nine years.

White Australia policy was an immigration restriction act that came into law in 1901, designed to limit non-British migration to Australia. It was emboldened after World War II.

white sails refers to the first white men arriving and coming ashore in sailing ships.

wiltjas are shelters made by the Pitjantjatjara and other Aboriginal peoples.

Wood and Water Rattler was an early name for the original Ghan trains from Adelaide.

Wright, Thomas (Tom) (1902–1981) was a sheet-metal worker and trade union official. He corresponded with Olive and secured her a small pension. His book, *New Deal for the Aborigines* (1939), is said to be written in Olive's voice! Olive first became friends with his wife Mary Wright.

Yunmaji Waterhole is on Warlpiri country. In 1933, Olive described the place as 'a delight'.

Notes

Olive Muriel Pink: Her radical and idealistic life seeks a middle ground between an accurate scholarly presentation of Olive Pink and a personal interpretation of her life. I had the invaluable opportunity to spend a few days with Olive Pink's private papers at the AIATSIS Library in Canberra, as well as time at the South Australia Museum Library in Adelaide and the Northern Territory Library in Parliament House, Darwin. I have spent several periods in Alice Springs over the years, watching the development of Olive's garden.

However, I rely mainly on secondary sources with respect to references, dialogue and Olive's richly worded insights. Scholars including Julie Marcus and Gillian Ward have had the opportunity to study Olive in more detail and for that I respect and thank them.

The following references are noted in good faith. The integrity of the meaning and intent are in line with the sources consulted. Dialogue without notes is intuited from my research.

Foreword

1. N. Underhill 2007, p. 236.
2. Admittedly it was summer and extremely hot and the café and museum were closed.
3. Olive was an advocate of humanistic anthropology to avoid the sterile dehumanisation which marked most anthropological writing of the time. 'The intellects had dehumanised the people they were studying.' (Stanner 1968)
4. Term coined by W.E.H. Stanner for Boyer lecture 1968.
5. Ibid.
6. Marcus 1993.

1

1. Kunanyi – a mountain in Hobart, Tasmania, previously known as Mt Wellington. Gazetted (1913) *Aboriginal & Dual Naming Policy,* ADNP, Tasmania 2013.
2. W.W. Spicer, *A Handbook of*

the Plants of Tasmania. Her father's friend A.T. Bell gave it to her in 1896, when she was aged twelve and already showing an interest in native plants.

3. From Lewis Carroll's *Alice in Wonderland*, a childhood favourite of Olive. She kept it with her throughout her life.

4. Two books being read by the informed people at this time. *Early Tasmania* (1902) by J.B. Walker. Walker's niece Miss Sarah Walker was Olive's headmistress. The Walkers, as Quakers, had come to investigate the persecution of the Aboriginal people. *Tasmania's Vanished Race* (1924) by Professor Frederic Wood Jones. Dr William Crowther gave Olive a copy.

5. Letter of reference from Lucien Dechaineux, 8 April 1910, in Olive Pink Collection MS2368 in the Australia Institute of Aboriginal and Torres Strait Islanders Studies Library (AIATSIS), Canberra, hereafter abbreviated MS 2368.

6. Mary Walker (sister of Sarah) studied at the Slade School in London and returned to Hobart with an interesting European collection of art. There was already a collection of Aboriginal artefacts by Mary Walker's father, an English Quaker who studied the welfare and treatment of Aboriginal peoples and of transported convicts around 1830.

7. Marcus 2001, p. 28.

8. Olive would be aware of leaving her secure world but as the Japanese word for crisis is made up of two characters – danger and opportunity, Olive sees the risk as worthwhile – a significant characteristic throughout her life.

9. Marcus 2001, pp. 28–29. P&O *Morea* Hobart to Perth.

10. Letter from Olive Pink to Muriel Pink, 19 November 1943, private collection.

11. Marcus 2001, p. 28

12. Ibid. p. 28 (*Bedford School Magazine*, December 1913).

13. Propaganda posters. World War I 1914–1918. (416,809 Australians enlisted.) *Posters on exhibition: Old Parliament House,* Canberra, 2008.

14. Harold Southern's paintings given to her were *Daffodils* (lost) and *Paper Bark Trees* painted on the banks of the Swan River in Kings Park, Perth. It was with her in Alice Springs when she died, along with the photo of

Harold Southern. It is now held in the Olive Pink Collection at the University of Tasmania Museum and Art Gallery. It was donated by the OPBG in 2007.

15. HMS *Ascanius* bound for Egypt, left Fremantle, Western Australia, 1914.

16. Olive was inspired by a lecture given by the artist and architect John Sultan.

17. Harold was mortally wounded at Gallipoli on 2 May 1915, aged 25, with his brother, Arthur. His grave in France is registered at the Australian War Memorial. Service No. 6638.

18. Her distress at Harold's death caused a strained heart valve. It weakened her heart, leaving her with a heart murmur for life. Medication, Dr Harriet Biffin's Tonic, was used for the rest of her life for breathlessness and lassitude. After Olive's death a clipping from a paper, 18 November 1975, 'The Romance of the Century: The story of Miss Pink and the Captain she loved for 60 years'. Another article in *Sunday Telegraph* 12 October 1975, p. 9, headlined 'Woman roamed desert to forget love killed at Gallipoli'.

19. *The Paper Bark Trees*, painting by Harold.

20. The League of Nations was the first worldwide intergovernmental organisation whose principal mission was to maintain world peace. It began in 1920 following the Paris Peace Conference that ended World War I in 1919.

21. Daisy May Bates – see Glossary. Later became a welfare worker and anthropologist among Aborigines and a lifelong student of Australian Aboriginal culture and society. Olive and Daisy met at the ANZAAS Conference 1926.

22. Ooldea – see Glossary.

2

1. The Tea and Sugar Rattler – see Glossary.

2. Marcus 2001, p. 36.

3. This is Olive's first encounter with the Pitjantjatjara peoples.

4. A name of endearment given to Daisy Bates, by the Indigenous people.

5. Marcus 2001, p. 31.

6. Ibid.

7. Ward 2018, p. 54.

8. Daisy Bates could communicate in 122 dialects. (Wikipedia).

9. Marcus 2001, p. 35.

10. Notes by Olive Pink

describing her stay at Ooldea, MS 2368.

11. Marcus 2001, p. 35.

12. This was a secure job and utilised her drawing and painting skills. It is thought she designed posters for the trains.

13. Olive's mother died in Sydney, 8 June 1927.

14. Olive proved throughout her life that at the point of crises she always saw the possible. Maybe her father taught her this as he read *Alice in Wonderland* to her. 'Fiddly-dee' Alice would say and push on.

15. Marcus 2001, p. 25. Inspired by her school motto 'Follow after truth', which had a strong impact on her, making her, she said, 'such a difficult person to deal with'. Feint inscribed around the bookplate the words 'Simplicity, Beauty, Honour, Truth'.

16. Marcus 2001, p. 80.

17. Ibid., p. 40. Noted: Dr. H. Wardlaw, Lecturer, Sydney University; W.W. Thorpe, ethnologist, Australian Museum, and Mr Towle.

18. The first meeting of the Anthropological Society of New South Wales, 16 October 1928, with Olive a founding member.

19. Marcus 2001, p. 40, *Mankind*, 19 October 1931.

3

1. Brooks, an old prospector who was speared by Aborigines in payback for stealing Aboriginal women. This triggered the Coniston Massacre. 'Nugget' Morton was involved in conflict with the Aborigines in the Sandover Massacre, in which 100 or more Aborigines were either shot or poisoned by strychnine, after it was alleged they stole cattle.

2. Daily rations kept the Indigenous families dependent. Olive will later write that this caused lethargy.

3. Pascoe 2014, p. 17. 'The fertility encouraged by careful husbandry of the soil over thousands of years was destroyed in just a few seasons. eg in Victoria the lush yam pastures disappeared as soon as sheep grazed on them as the dentition of sheep allowed them to eat growth right to the ground, destroying the basal leaves.' Inland had already suffered with the white man's interference. The Indigenous were unable to move around as they had in oral history. They were being crippled.

4. The Coniston massacre took place near the Coniston cattle

station in the then Territory of Central Australia from 14 August to 18 October 1928. The last known officially sanctioned massacre of Indigenous Australians as part of what is termed Australian Frontier Wars. (Reynolds 2013)

5. In 1968, more than 30 years on, W.E.H. Stanner will make his voice heard in the Boyer Lectures where he coins the term 'The great Australian silence' and speaks of the white-washing of history.

6. Pastor A.P. Elkin lived at Morpeth Theological College. He wrote an article of concern for the Indigenous tribes after a journey he took into the North inland. It articulated what Olive was thinking and feeling. It was the beginning of a long correspondence.

7. A result of her job with the Department of Railways.

8. Oodnadatta, the old terminus – end of the line until 1929.

9. Professor J.B. Cleland from the Adelaide Museum was very helpful. She was introduced by letter from her family friend from Tasmania, William Crowther. Cleland assisted her plans over the years.

10. Sometimes called the Wood and Water rattler.

11. Edwards Crossing Depot. Here she planned to stay for a few days to sketch plants and meet the local people.

12. Marcus 2001, p. 45 from diary of Horrie Simpson.

13. MS 2368. Letter Oliver Muriel Pink, hereafter abbreviated OMP, to nieces.

14. Marcus 2001, p.48. In later years, Pastor Elkin insisted that after she had left Sydney his plans changed and he had not been able to advise her. Letter OMP to JBC, 17 May 1932

15. Ibid.

16. MS 2368.

4

1. Robert Manne.

2. Marcus 2001, pp. 48–49 (adapted for dialogue).

3. Alice Springs called Stuart until 1933 and Mparntwe for thousands of years. The rail line from Oodnadatta to Alice opened in 1933.

4. The Overland Telegraph Line linking Adelaide and Darwin began the settlement.

5. Darwin is the seat of governance for the Northern Territory. Situated at the most northern port on the Timor Sea.

6. The frontier in the 30s was

described by W.E.H. Stanner as 'the rotting frontier' as many of the preconditions of the traditional cultures were gone. No longer could the tribal people confidently depend on nature.

7. Olive Pink left hundreds of letters and articles. She strongly criticised government officials, missionaries and pastoralists, making uncompromising demands. Her constant badgering of politicians resulted in her being investigated by ASIO as a Communist sympathiser.

8. Mick Dow Dow and his brother Bruno. Both were Indigenous 'anthropologists'. Like Olive, curious about their culture, they were curious about her too and ready to inform her. They knew of Spencer and Gillen's *The Arunta* and were impressed that Olive carried a copy.

9. Hermannsburg Mission – see Glossary. When Olive visited Hermannsburg, Pastor Albrecht, a Lutheran minister, was in charge.

10. Pastor Albrecht is friendly. He informs Olive he knows that a pastoralist called Braitling has applied for a lease of land in this area.

11. Tjurunga, a sacred stone used in ritual.

12. Olive was shocked to realise that Albrecht did not make any room for a spirituality of the Arrernte. He saw all rituals only as curiosities and not part of a deep spiritual understanding of life.

13. Albert Namatjira – see Glossary.

5

1. Little did Olive know at this time that Mick Dow Dow and his brother Bruno and their interest in working with her was the foundation on which her anthropological research would be built.

2. The words 'rotting frontier' which will be used by the well known anthropologist W.E.H. (Ted) Stanner in the Boyer Lectures, more than thirty years later in 1968.

3. A phrase named and proclaimed by Stanner in 1968 in the Boyer Lectures.

4. Marcus 2001, p. 52, from an unpublished manuscript.

5. Olive wrote to many, including letters and articles for papers, with a perseverance and skill to lobby. She did not hesitate to drop names of Darwin contacts.

6. She spoke often at the NSW

Anthropological Society meeting. Her unacceptable views were contrary to the conventional reality giving cause for her to be alienated.

7. Olive Pink at the Anthropology Society meeting foreseeing the need to protect an area of the Warlpiri people. Adapted from reading MS 2368 Papers of OMP.

8. Marcus 2001, p. 62

9. From diaries MS 2368.

10. Imagined conversation of the decision-making at the meeting.

11. OMP letter to William Crowther MS 2368.

12. Raymond Firth, an academic article, Sydney University. 1928.

13. Letter, 1928. Firth to OMP MS 2368

14. OMP to Cleland, April 1932. See also Rouse 1998 for study of the impact of rationing.

15. Marcus 2001, p. 62. Crowther to OMP.

16. Ibid. p. 61. Olive was still uneasy because of his perceived betrayal on the early journey inland.

17. Ibid. p. 62.

18. Ibid.

19. ANZAAS Conference 1932 held in Sydney.

20. Imagined thoughts from reading her diaries MS 2368 Diaries.

21. Ibid.

22. Adapted from anthropological notes MS 2368.

23. Ted Strehlow is referring to Hermannsburg Mission.

24. Adapted from Letter OMP to Crowther.

25. Ibid.

6

1. From letter OMP to Crowther 1933.

2. Ibid.

3. Anthropologists Norman Tindale and Herbert Hale.

4. Reconstructed from reading diaries and notes MS 2368.

5. Olive remembered telling missionary friends, the Kramers, of her plans at the ANZAAS dinner party and feels they betrayed her by telling Strehlow, and that he got in before her.

6. Jim and Charlie Dow Dow. Olive worked with these two brothers but more with Bruno and Mick and their families. In the later years, they all visited her at Home Hut often.

7. Ilpalentye country. As the crow flies, this country is not more than thirty-five miles from Alice Springs. A rich ancestral land for Arrernte society. They covered 100 miles in this round journey to complete her thesis.

8. Marcus 2001, p. 72.

9. Olive studied the anthropological idea of kinship, fascinated with its philosophy.

10. Water was scarce and European settlers had already driven cattle across the country, had actually blasted the Ilpalentye soakage to make it bigger and had broken the natural basin beneath the sand that held the water. As a result, the spring dried up in dry times.

11. At AIATSIS, I was immersed in nineteen boxes of catalogued notes, diaries, articles, lectures and letters part of Olive's legacy.

12. 'Bright Star' by John Keats, English Romantic poet, (1795–1821).

13. The Arrernte word for corkwood bark.

14. OMP to Crowther, 5 July 1933, Tasmanian Collection.

15. Caledon Bay is in north-east Arnhem Land.

16. Headlines of papers, 'Government prepares Punitive expedition against Blacks', *Melbourne Herald*, 2 September 1933; 'Expedition ready to punish Blacks. Fighting and bloodshed fear', *The Sun*, 2 September 1933; 'The world is judging us', *The Herald*, 5 September 1933

17. Reynolds 2018, p. 175. Rev. C.E.C. Lefroy in *London Anti-Slave Reporter* observed '"punitive" is a mild description for slaughtering expeditions that have long been the established custom – and it is only now, at long last that the Australian people have become conscious of their enormity'.

18. *Sydney Morning Herald*. The campaign of protest began on 15 August. Letters and telegrams poured into Canberra from churches, missionary, organisations, feminist groups, unions, pacifists, Labour and Liberal party. It showed Coniston was still fresh in peoples minds and change was sought. Telegram from Archbishop Daniel Mannix 5/9/33 to Prime Minister Lyons: 'With, I hope a majority of Australians, I regard the punitive expedition with grave misgivings and the possible result with horror.'

19. *Canberra Times*, 1 September 1933.

20. Reynolds 2018, p. 176, OMP to Prime Minister Lyons, telegram.

21. Ibid. *Sydney Morning Herald*, 5 September 1933, Stanner writes, 'many people are agitated and dismayed at the prospect of a punitive expedition – now we call it 'instrument of savage injustice'. A.P. Elkin writes, 'a tradition of giving the natives a lesson is abhorrent to many thinking Australians'.

22. The High Commissioner in London (SM Bruce) writes to Lyons and by 5 September the government is in retreat.

23. Reynolds 2018, p. 176.

7

1. Adapted from correspondence and conversation. Olive wrote many essays on totemism in her effort to grapple with the philosophy of this society and culture.

2. Adapted conversation of Elkin's suggestion to Olive.

3. Olive had to argue with Elkin about the grant. She was given £300 for the year, but knew the men got £250 for three months. She had to write and beg for more money.

4. From letter OMP to Crowther.

5. Telegrams were not private and letters were handled and generated gossip.

6. Marcus 2001, pp. 86–87.

7. Ibid. p. 88

8. The Coniston Massacre had been instigated from here. This story told in later years demonstrates her angst.

9. Adapted from Olive's diaries MS 2368. The traditional owners of this area around Doreen Station are the Warlpiri people, who received Native Title Recognition in 2014.

10. From diaries MS 2368.

11. She is respected by her *Peltharre* affiliation from her Arrernte work. This is translated into the Warlpiri equivalent, *Napaljarri*.

12. She had promised specimens of plants for Professor Cleland's Adelaide Museum and butterflies for the Australian Museum, Sydney.

13. Marcus 2001, p. 96. Olive collected about 700 words towards a dictionary.

14. Ibid. p. 99, letter OMP to Crowther.

15. Ibid. pp. 98–99.

16. Ibid.

17. Ibid.

18. from notes MS 2368.

8

1. Pink, Olive, 'The Landowners of the northern division of the Aranda tribe, Central Australia', *Oceania* 6 (3): 275–305.

2. Marcus 2001, p. 180. Olive is unsafe in the desert – Strehlow advises her research grant be terminated.

3. Letter OMP to Crowther.

4. Bob made the deal with the elder, Japaljarri.

5. Marcus 2001, p. 129 The children, when grown up, said Olive was the first white woman they had seen and she reassured them about things including planes, a new thing in the sky.

6. Letter OMP to Crowther.

7. Quote from Japaljarri sited in Marcus 2001, OMP 31/1/35, Japaljarri's way of showing how he would miss her.

9

1. Secular sanctuary, in Olive's vision, was where the people could develop at their own pace without being exploited as cheap labour or indoctrinated by missionaries.

2. Elkin was now a very powerful figure, head of the Anthropology Department, editor of the anthropology journal *Oceania* and a member of all the important boards and societies.

3. As in note 1, this is to be an absolute reserve for the native tribes inhabiting it. According to Olive Pink, 'a place where they can call their souls and bodies their own'.

4. Frederic Wood-Jones published a call for just such a reserve. He was a highly respected academic who worked at South Australia's Museum. He spoke of this in a series on ABC radio and published a book: 'It is much to be hoped that before it is too late, a more enlightened policy will prevail, and at long last a redeemed Australian reputation of dealing with the people upon whose ancestral hunting grounds she grows her wheat and wool'. Wood-Jones, ABC, 1934.

5. It means lobbying the government of the day. To have a chance, she needs the backing of the ANZAAS Congress in Melbourne, to publish her Arrernte work and have the ANRC on side to give her a new grant. Finally, her vision is to be administrator of this created reserve. It needed to be large

enough to support the traditional way of life and to have its natural waters preserved from the depredations of stock, which not only competed for water with people but fouled the waterholes.

6. Marcus 2001, p. 145. Olive believed cultural contact lay where coloniser law met Aboriginal law and secondly in predatory sexual relations on the frontier.

7. This allegation spread widely throughout Central Australia and has never been laid to rest.

8. Marcus 2001, p. 157. Calling up traditional stereotypes of feminine ineptitude and masculine sovereignty.

9. Lewis Carroll.

10. Marcus 2001, p. 150. Anyone reading the 1997 report on the Stolen Generation, *Bringing them Home,* will find many tragic stories of traumatised Aboriginal 'shells' and the system of missions and 'protection' which produced them and which Olive railed against. She saw so clearly what was actually happening.

11. ANRC Australian National Research Council.

12. OMP to her childhood friend Violet.

13. Marcus 2001, p. 180.

14. Ibid. p. 161. Olive faced the brunt all her life of a misogynist anthropological culture and ailing injustice which is historically noted by other women anthropology students and in many other career paths sought by women. (Two women students of Elkin give up, two others leave for work in London, others are marginalised.)

15. From diaries MS 2368. Stormy Campbell worked odd jobs around Fogarty's garage. He maintained and restored cars. Olive says, 'he was a very good driver, plucky and genial, kindly and straight'. Noted one time as her 'trustworthy driver'. He also searched out and acquired the old green Chevrolet when she had a Quaker donation to purchase her truck.

16. Letter Crowther to OMP.

17. Marcus 2001, p. 192. It is a shock to realise the decision to cancel her grant was done while Elkin was away. (He was attending a conference in Honolulu and could not argue her case.) The ANRC's members tried to control her by making her dependent on small monthly payments, a system

unsuited to a situation in which large amounts had to be paid in advance for planning, wages, transport and bulk rations.

18. Ibid. She heard about the telegram before she received it and being called Pink added to the anger. 'Pink is refused further grants and recalled from the field.' The acrimonious exchanges of telegrams with the ANRC meant that her affairs and 'disgrace' were publicly and widely discussed in town. She felt humiliated and embarrassed.

19. Ibid. p. 199. She wrote to Elkin, 'Why should one be recalled by a public telegram and on the obviously ludicrous excuse and lie of being anxious about my health and safety. I am far safer with Stone Age men than with the Sydney ANRC.'

20. Her reply to Elkin, 'Do give up pretence and be an open (and not a semi-covert enemy) your "with all good wishes" is more a policy stunt and insincere to a degree I prefer stone age knife fights to the stabbing in the back tactics of the ANRC... Yours disgustedly, O.M. Pink.'

21. Sydney to Hobart, probably the cruise ship *Ormiston*, 28 March 1937.

22. Ward, p. 78, cited letter OMP to her nieces in 1944: 'I have designed and painted a diorama of an Aboriginal family group using real artefacts in the display with weapons and cooking utensils in their hands. They found me a valuable resource for them while I was there. I wonder if it is still on display.'

23. Olive's views were out of step with those of her colleagues. Her concern with secrecy and the honouring of promises set her right outside the boundaries of professional acceptability. Her views are remarkably in sympathy with those prevailing thirty to forty years after her death.

24. Olive sails from Hobart, Tasmania for the last time, June 1938, on the *Zealandia*.

25. Marcus 2001, p. 204.

10

1. Her wish to do welfare work was prevented. The governors and protectors were suspicious of 'the dangerous outspoken Miss Pink', and refused her access to the government or missionary reserves. They were afraid she could insight discontent or worse still, report

appalling conditions to the media. Once when she was desperate to see the ailing Bruno, she said they could take her blindfolded so she couldn't see the conditions.

2. Marcus 2001, p. 219. Sheetmetal Workers Union Fund organised by Tom Wright, (Vice President of the Labour Council of NSW). Olive's connection with Tom of course made the governors and ASIO even more suspicious of her Communist tendencies.

3. Ibid. p. 253. That Olive Pink had lived out among the Warlpiri was more than sufficient to ensure that later in the self-consciously modern town she could be assigned a place among the 'local characters' who represented the frontier legends of the town's past and a place in the pantheon of 'old timers'.

4. Ibid. p. 247. Olive's insistence on the communal and cooperative structure of the community reflected her understanding of what she called 'the natural socialism of Warlpiri civilisation'. Tom Wright was proposing ways to make her vision viable .He wrote suggesting the Warlpiri men organise themselves as a labour cooperative and to pool resources.

5. It is a desert oak tree – a type of casuarina. Because she was on Crown land which had not been made over to either pastoralists or missions, she needed no permit to live there and no one could stop her welfare work.

6. MS 2368. Letters from OMP to nieces.

7. Marcus 2001, p. 241, An elder today, Iris Long Nangala, one of the children of those years, when interviewed said, 'My mother and father, all of the Warlpiri mob looked after Talkinjiya, We walked around country, but still came back to see her. We hunted for goanna and bush tucker and shared it with her.

8. For a 'secular sanctuary' Olive had sourced out the area, the Granites, and its waterhole now known as *Papinya*. It was Crown land and she decided this would be the best spot for her lease of land to form a safe haven for the Warlpiri and provide an opportunity to demonstrate the value of a secular reserve. While she waited for the red tape and bungles of leasing the land, she lived at Thompson's Rock Hole for the next few years.

9. The bombing of Darwin, also known as the Battle of Darwin, on 19 February 1942, was the largest single attack ever mounted by a foreign power on Australia. The gravity of it was under blanket censorship at the time.

10. Ward, pp. 87–90, adapted from letter OMP to nieces.

11. *The Northern Standard*, 24 March 1950. Segregation refers to the twentieth-century system of removing Indigenous people onto reserves and missions, often in the guise of *protecting* Indigenous people. This policy involved high levels of government interference into Indigenous lives and culture.

12. A.P. Elkin warns her of this.

13. MS 2368 from letters adapted.

14. Ward, p. 96, and from papers MS 2368, letter OMP to nieces.

15. Newspapers on Hiroshima atomic bomb explosion in Japan, August 1945.

16. Newspapers cited from Trove.

17. Boulton 1987. 'One of the worst features of the contact between the advancing white race and the dark race in Australia has been the lack of food provided for the Aborigines after their natural food has been seriously diminished or lost to them.'

18. Food depots later renamed ration depots. To prevent widespread starvation during the time from 1920s to 1960s, rations were provided by the government. Rations became the vehicle of control and created an inevitable dependency. (Rowe 1998) This dependency became lethal through starvation. (Boulton) Berndt and Berndt 1987, p. 271 documented an entrenched system of oppression to the point of slavery, with widespread malnutrition and a devastatingly high level of maternal and infant mortality. Publication of their report was suppressed by Elkin, who considered that it would do more harm than good, thus the Berndts' report was not published until forty years later.

19. Pascoe 2014, p. 17 notes, 'Farmers noted the alarming drop in productivity over a mere handful of years as cattle and sheep ate out the croplands and compacted the light soils…the run-off accelerated and different grasses dominated.'

20. This final trek into Alice Springs has been documented by a teacher for a local school as a heroine's journey.

11

1. The tent was set on the common at Gregory Terrace, an area of crown land set aside to benefit the local community.

2. MS 2368. Letter OMP to Tom Wright. Olive was also outraged that since the war many of the able-bodied men were sent where there was a labour shortage far from their own country and could not return.

3. The 1946 Pilbara strike was a landmark strike by Indigenous Australian pastoral workers in the Pilbara region of Western Australia for human rights recognition and payment of fair wages and working conditions.

4. Ward p. 99. Afghan cameleers in Australia, also known as 'Afghans' or 'Ghans', were camel drivers who worked in Outback Australia from the 1860s to the 1930s.

5. Olive Pink put up signs around town advertising her Museum. The local tourist officer would send people down to visit her.

6. Cynthia Nolan diary – she called it a very pleasant visit.

7. Reg Harris, *Olive Muriel Pink, Angel of Protest, 1930s–1970s*, from Legendary Territorian, Alice Springs, Harris 2007 p. 44. (cited Ward pp. 100–101).

8. Marcus, p. 230. Olive was critical of the disconnect between the British Legal System and Aboriginal Law and language.

12

1. Ward, p. 103. Dr. John Hargrave later wrote, 'She was a prolific letter writer, indeed it was through her letters that she expressed frankly and fearlessly her opinion in graphic detail. She said exactly what she meant. And ruffled many feathers.' Olive says after many visits and much correspondence, 'You are like a grandson that I advise.' Yabbula to Yabbula: Letters Olive Pink and John Hargrave from private collection of letters.' (Trove)

2. Ibid. p. 99.

3. The newspapers claimed the White Australian Policy was a divisive tactic compared with the 'iron curtain' in Europe. *The Sunday Times,* 16 March 1947.

4. This relationship was frowned on as the White Australia Policy was seen as important in town.

5. MS 2368.

6. Ibid.

7. Marcus 2001, pp. 278–9. (Albert Namatjira and Olive met in Alice Springs regularly.)

8. MS 2368.

9. Letter OMP to nieces.

10. Marcus 2001, p. 270. Letter OMP to Crowther 2/10/1959.

11. Ibid. pp. 270–271 and MS 2368.

12. Ibid. p. 278, Telegram to Minister Paul Hasluck.

13. Finnane, Kiernan ed., *The Alice Springs News,* 6 July 2016, writes, 'even his estate was taken up by white men and until a few years ago had not been returned'. Finnane proclaimed, 'I can hear the ghost of Olive Pink in this story!' PS 15/10/2017: Dick Smith has intervened, bought out Legend Press and facilitated the return of copyright to the Namatjira family after 56 years of deprivation.

14. OMP to Minister of Territories Paul Hasluck. Olive was prevented from visiting as she was deemed 'communist' and her influence undesirable.

15. Marcus 2001, pp. 272–3. Hasluck later apologised, saying he was at a conference in Perth.

16. Ibid.

17. Ibid.

18. Ibid, p. 270, OMP to Hasluck. John McDouall Stuart.

19. To lose her Home Hut where she had worked so hard, means losing her home and her income from her garden. To lose her job means more loss of income and loss of the courtroom space for writing.

20. From poem 'Thunder raining poison' by Ali Cobby Eckermann.

21. Maralinga in the remote western areas of South Australia, the home of the Maralinga Tjarutja, a southern Pitjantjatjara people. Maralinga was the site of the British nuclear tests in the 1950s.

22. From poem 'Thunder raining poison' by Ali Cobby Eckermann.

13

1. In 1955 the Acting Governor (Reginald Marsh) supplied Olive with an Occupational Licence for half an acre and the right to buy her Home Hut, which she'd lived in for over nine years. The Welfare Branch

to dismantle the hut for five pounds.

2. Letter OMP to nieces.

3. MS 2368.

4. Ibid., letters OMP to nieces

5. Ibid.

6. Ward, pp. 105–107 After writing many letters and much lobbying an area of fourteen acres was gazetted on 23 September 1956.

7. Ibid. p. 107.

8. Water-wise garden. Olive uses the native arid plants that are more drought-resistant. An arid garden is one that has plants which survive with under ten inches of rainfall a year. Olive finds every way to channel and conserve the few inches of rain that are received.

9. OMP letter to Crowther 1959.

10. Ward, pp. 114–115 and map cited in MS 2368 of trees with names of men in power.

11. Assimilation Policy 1951 – a policy of absorbing Aboriginal people into white society through the process of removing children from their families. The ultimate intent of this policy was the destruction of Aboriginal society. The Assimilation Policy was formally abolished by the Commonwealth Government in 1973, in favour of self-management by Indigenous people.

12. Sir Paul Hasluck told this story on Radio ABC. 'I visited her on several occasions and could never restrain a curious glance at my tree and felt suitably gratified if I saw that "Mr Hasluck" was being watered regularly (From 'Miss Pink, love story', *Northern Territory Newsletter*, July 1975, pp. 4–9.

13. Ward, p. 110.

14. Ibid., p. 107. Olive was an experienced gardener by the time she was curator of the Flora Reserve. She had successfully created and tended gardens around her homes all her life in a great diversity of environments from the heat of the desert to the cool temperate forest on Mt Wellington (Kunanyi) in Tasmania.

15. Ibid., p. 109.

14

1. Pascoe 2014, pp. 13–15 Pascoe writes, 'The conventional framework denied Aboriginal culture its real place. The first settlers were describing a land which could make a profit. The

pioneers had their preconception of the frontier… so powerful they skew their observation to that prejudice.'

2. Marcus 2001, p. 2.

3. Ibid., p. 294.

4. Ibid., p. 108.

5. Ibid., p. 240, p. 261.

15

1. Marcus 2001, p. 298.

2. Ibid.

3. Her books and family photographs went to her three nieces. Her Aboriginal artefacts were bequeathed to the Tasmania Museum and University and her Anthropological writings are now held at the Australian Institute of Aboriginal and Torres Strait Islander Studies in Canberra. (AIATSIS.) Her two paintings went to the Tasmanian Museum and Art Gallery. As she wished, the painting *Paper Barks* by Harold Southern was with her when she died and was given by the Olive Pink Gardens in 2004 to the University of Tasmania. She donated 200 of her own botanical paintings and sketches 1912–1960 to the University of Tasmania Library.

4. Gillian Ward mounted an exhibition of Olive Pink's paintings in 2004. University of Tasmania Library and Tasmanian Museum and Art Gallery (TMAG), located in Hobart, Tasmania.

5. MS 2368, Diary notes 17/6/1972.

6. Seven Sisters – The Star Dreaming story of the Seven Sisters is one of the most widely distributed ancient stories of Aboriginal Australia. The songline for this story covers more than half the width of the continent, from deep in the Central Desert out to the West Coast. The songline travels through many different language groups and different sections of the narrative are recognised in different parts of the country.

7. In our visit to the Garden in March 2020, this stillness was very real and we were impressed how her wish, her mission, is being upheld.

8. MS 2368. Adapted from diaries. Olive always believed when the truth was known, justice would inevitably follow. (Marcus 1993).

9. Attempts had been made with council wanting control.

Epilogue

1. Ward 2018, p. 117.
2. Last Will and Testament of Miss Olive Muriel Pink 31 August 1973. Olive loved violets and had two friends called Violet from her young days. The flowers meant friendship to her.
3. Marcus 1991.

Bibliography

AIATSIS Papers of Olive Muriel Pink 1884–1975 Series 1 Manuscripts: Series 11 Printed material. 19 boxes. Stanner Reading Room, Canberra, ACT MS 2368.

Andrews, Munya 2019, *Journey into Dreamtime*. Ultimate World Publishing.

Araluen Centre Alice Springs, *Fierce – the Meeting of Miss Pink*, November 2002 Music.

Berndt R. and C. Berndt 1987, *End of an Era. Aboriginal Labour in the Northern Territory*. Canberra, Australian Institute of Aboriginal Studies.

Blueprint for Living, ABC, Dr Victoria Grieve-Williams, 2019.

Boulton, John 1987, *Aboriginal Children, History and Health: Beyond Social Determinants* (in Berndt and Berndt, p. 271)

Bringing them Home: Report of the National Inquiry into the separation of Aboriginal and Torres Strait Islander children from their families, April 1997.

Hargrave, John ed. *Yabbula to Yabbula: Letters Olive Pink and John Hargrave* from private collection.

Harris, Reg 2007, *Olive Muriel Pink: Alice Springs, Angel of Protest 1930–1970* from Legendary Territorians.

Hasluck, Paul Papers in range (1925–1989) MS 5274 National Library of Australia

Heathcote, Angela, 'Seventeen Incredible Australian Women in Botany', *Australian Geographic* March 2018.

— 'Olive Pink is Australia's very own Georgia O'Keefe', *Australian Geographic.* November 2018.

Hill, Barry 2002, *Broken Song: T.G.H. Strehlow and Aboriginal Possession.* Random House.

Kilgariff, Fran AM 2018, *Miss Pink: An unforgettable woman from Guide to the Garden.*

Latz, Peter 2014, *Olive Pink Botanical Garden: a globally unique treasure.* OP Garden.

— 2018, *Olive Pink Botanic Garden: A globally unique treasure, from Guide to the Garden.*

Lyndon, Jane & Ryan, Lyndall 2018, *Remembering the Myall Creek Massacre.* New South Publishing.

Mahood, Kim 2016, *Position Doubtful: Mapping landscapes and memories.* Scribe.

Manne, Robert, *W.E.H. Stanner: Making Trouble: Essays Against the New Australian Complacency*, Quarterly Essay, No. 43.

Marcus, Julie 1989, *An Introduction to Reading Olive Pink,* The Olive Pink Society Bulletin 1 pp.11–13.

— 1991, *Yours Truly, Olive Pink. Collection of Letters.* Olive Pink Society, Canberra.

— 1993, *The Beauty, Simplicity and Honour of Truth: Pink in the 1940s* (in the above anthology). MUP.

— (ed.) 1993, *First in their Field: Women and Australian Anthropology*. MUP.

— 2001, *The Indomitable Miss Pink: A life in Anthropology.* UNSW Press.

Moriarty, Ros 2011, *Listening to Country: A journey to the heart of what it means to belong.* Allen & Unwin.

Nicholls, Christine Judith 'Dreamtime and The Dreaming – an introduction', *The Conversation*, 23 January 2014.

Oodgeroo Noonuccal *My People* third edition 1990.

Pascoe, Bruce 2014, *Dark Emu: Black Seeds, agriculture or accident.* Magabala Books.

Perkins, Rachael 2020, *End of Silence,* Boyer Lectures Series, ABC.

Pink, Olive, 'Spirit Ancestors in a Northern Aranda Horde Country', December 1933. Reprinted courtesy of *Oceania* Vol. IV, No. 2, pp. 176–186. Bulletin of Olive Pink Society Vol. 1, No.1, February 1989.

Reynolds, Henry 2013, *Forgotten War.* New South Books.

— 2018, *The Whispering in our Hearts Revisited.* New South Books.

Rolls, Eric 2011, *A Million Wild Acres.* Hale & Iremonger.

Rouse, Tim 1998, *White Flour, White Power:From Rations to Citizenship in Central Australia.* Cambridge University Press.

Spenser, B. & Gillen, F. 1899, *The Native Tribes of Central Australia.* Dover.

Stanner, W.E.H. 1968, *After the Dreaming: black and white Australians – an Anthropologist's view,* Boyer Lectures Series 1968 (The Great Australian Silence) Sydney, ABC.

— 1979. *White Man Got No Dreaming,* 1938–1973, ANU, Research Papers 1979.

Stewart, Peter 2007, *Demons at Dusk.* Temple House.

The Botanical Gardens

Newsletter, for botanical gardens of Australia and New Zealand. No. 3, July 2002.

Underhill, N. (ed.) 2007, *Nolan on Nolan: Sidney Nolan in his own words*. Viking Press.

Ward, Gillian 2018, *Olive Pink, A Life in Flowers: Artist, Activist & Gardener*. Hardie Grant Books.

Wright, Judith 1996, 'Two Dreamtimes', from *A Human Pattern: Selected Poems*. ETT.